Structures and forces
Stages 1 & 2

A Unit for teachers

Published for the Schools Council by
Macdonald Educational, London and Milwaukee

First published in Great Britain 1972 by
Macdonald Educational Ltd
Holywell House, Worship Street
London EC2A 2EN

Macdonald-Raintree Inc.
205 W. Highland Avenue
Malwaukee, Wisconsin 53203

Reprinted 1973, 1974 (with amendments), 1978

ISBN 0 356 04007 0

Library of Congress Catalog Card Number
77-82991

The chief author of this book:

Albert James   Deputy Project Director

The other members of the Science 5/13 team:

Len Ennever   Project Director

Wynne Harlen   Evaluator

Sheila Parker
Don Radford
Roy Richards
Mary Horn

Made and printed by Waterlow (Dunstable) Ltd

General preface

'Science 5/13' is a project sponsored jointly by the Schools Council, the Nuffield Foundation and the Scottish Education Department, and based at the University of Bristol School of Education. It aims at helping teachers to help children between the ages of five and thirteen years to learn science through first-hand experience using a variety of methods.

The Project produces books, that comprise Units dealing with subject-areas in which children are likely to conduct investigations. Some of these Units are supported by books of background information. These Units are linked by objectives that the Project team hopes children will attain through their work. The aims of the Project are explained in a general guide for teachers called *With objectives in mind*, which contains the Project's guide to Objectives for children learning science, reprinted at the back of each Unit.

Acknowledgements

The Project is deeply grateful to its many friends:
to the local education authorities who have
helped us work in their areas, to those of their staff
who, acting as area representatives, have borne
the heavy brunt of administering our trials, and to
the teachers, heads and wardens who have been
generous without stint in working with their
children on our materials. The books we have
written drew substance from the work they did
for us, and it was through their critical appraisal
that our materials reached their present form. For
guidance, we had our sponsors, our Consultative
Committee and, for support, in all our working,
the University of Bristol. To all of them we
acknowledge our many debts: their help has been
invaluable.

Metrication

This has given us a great deal to think about.
We have been given much good advice by
well-informed friends, and we have consulted
many reports by learned bodies. Following
the advice and the reports wherever possible
we have expressed quantities in metric units
with Imperial units afterwards in square
brackets if it seemed useful to state them so.

There are, however, some cases to which the
recommendations are difficult to apply. For
instance we have difficulty with units such as
miles per hour (which has statutory force in this
country) and with some Imperial units that are
still in current use for common commodities and,
as far as we know, liable to remain so for some
time. In these cases we have tried to use our
common sense, and, in order to make statements
that are both accurate and helpful to teachers
we have quoted Imperial measures followed by
the approximate metric equivalent in square
brackets if it seemed sensible to give them.

Where we have quoted statements made by
children, or given illustrations that are children's
work, we have left unaltered the units in which
the children worked—in any case some of
these units were arbitrary.

Contents

1 Introduction

Why a Unit on structures?

There seem to be at least three very good reasons why a Unit of work on structures should offer exciting possibilities in schools:

Children enjoy making structures

Early in their lives, children naturally start to build. It is not long after a child is first able to pick up objects that he puts one of them on top of another. Building bricks in a multitude of sizes and colours and constructive toys of similar nature, such as interlocking plastic shapes, become well-used toys. Even better loved for constructional work are cardboard boxes, step-ladders, broom-sticks and garden canes.

There seems to be some basic human urge to build a shelter. Children playing freely construct dens with branches and leaves among the shrubs, and juniors find great adventure in tree houses. An important element about a shelter construction is that it should be large enough to get inside, and some modern toy makers are producing constructional sections on a big enough scale for this. The book *Environmental Geometry* of the Nuffield Maths Project gives a good example of infant children building their own 'Wendy house' from shoeboxes. Soon the structures may develop beyond the basic shelter to models of cranes, bridges, cars and boats.

At a later stage, many boys develop an interest in more sophisticated engineering toys, like Meccano, and in structural model making—model aeroplanes, for instance. The girls join in when they are allowed to (see the Unit *Science from toys, Stages 1 & 2*).

Finally, great pleasure comes in helping to build structures for use: a tree house, a go-kart, a canoe, a telescope, a greenhouse or perhaps a swimming pool.

The environment is full of structures

The second point to recommend a Unit on structures is that there are so many around. Man is now so dependent on structures of all kinds in order to live the sort of life he does that children are surrounded by the most interesting structural objects, about which they are full of questions. Therefore, for work which we believe must start from observation of the environment, there is, ready to hand, around every child a wealth of starting points: houses, bridges, lamp posts, pylons, trees. One has not got to go very far to start looking and if only someone ventures to wonder why these things don't fall down or why the wind doesn't blow them over, science begins.

Work on structure leads to many new directions

Since structures are almost all built to assist some human activity (to live in, to cross a river, to carry electrical wires, to pick up radio waves, to hold gas and so on), looking at them and thinking about how they are made cannot be the end of the story. Consideration of the use to which they are put leads to much scientific interest, and, what is even better, to other 'subjects' and beyond the narrow idea of a subject at all to a wider enjoyment of learning and human culture.

The structure of a house must inevitably lead to

2

heating, lighting and furnishing, and to the people who live in the house. The study of the structure of a bridge, exciting in itself, is not really complete without looking at the traffic which goes over it, and few teachers would miss the opportunity of considering the great bridges of the world and of telling the life stories of the men who built the bridges. It really does not matter a bit whether the work is called science or geography or history at this stage.

Nor must we forget the structures that are made for the sheer enjoyment of making them, particularly when this has resulted in something intrinsically beautiful. We must look at sculpture of all kinds, in materials from paper to marble, and at the world's great architecture. That which is structurally sound and derives from a basic honesty and knowledge of the qualities of materials, is very often also beautiful. To help children to experience and appreciate this kind of beauty is something we must attempt from the start.

The idea of structure crosses the boundaries of the separate sciences. The rigidity of a tree trunk, the flexibility of a grass, the structures made by other animals than man, the stiffness of bones, and the way joints are built to turn and muscles to pull, are of vital interest. Structure is as important in living things as in man-made things.

Finally, reaching out beyond the limits set by our Project, it is easy to see the further steps in work on structure which will follow : work on the structure of matter, the chemistry, physics and biology of molecules and atoms.

Structure is interesting both in nature and in man-made things

2 Objectives are needed

. . . and he went out, not knowing whither he went (*Hebrews xi 8*)

It is now well established that science in the early stages of a child's life arises from active exploration of the environment. The work must be child-centred (that is, it should come from the child's own interest and questions) and should lead to active practical investigation. This is the way children learn best ; observation and experiment are essential stages of science too.

But one should not assume that this means setting out like Abraham. Some teachers may be able to do it, but many simply do not have the faith in their ability and background knowledge to cope with such an open situation. Some who have set out boldly have been disappointed to find no clear achievement or progress amongst the multitude of interests which arise, and so enthusiasm has fallen away.

Objectives are clearly needed. Objectives need not unduly structure work ; there are so many different ways of achieving them.

Objectives infants may have attained

Infants will be able to play with and appreciate a large variety of materials, not only water, sand and clay, but also fabrics, papers, cards, woods, metals, stones and plastics. They will have been able to see and feel them and will have used words to describe them. Probably, one property at a time, they will have made comparisons in a very simple way and considered, for example, smoothness, weight, hardness or colour.

Quite early they will have built with blocks or boxes and they will have sensed the effect of gravity and developed some idea about stability. Some will have tried to construct with other materials (paper and card, wood and fabrics particularly) and will have learnt by experience some of their limitations and possibilities. They will have looked at houses and cranes and trees, talked about them, made models and painted pictures.

So, perhaps, we could list some objectives attained as follows (even though these statements may appear rather coldly analytical for what goes on in infant schools).

Enjoyment in using all the senses for exploring and discriminating.   *1.04*

Willingness to collect material for observation and investigation.   *1.05*

Appreciation of the variety of living things and materials in the environment.   *1.21*

Awareness of the meaning of words which describe various types of quantity.   *1.31*

Ability to find answers to simple problems by investigation.   *1.41*

Ability to make comparisons in terms of one property or variable.   *1.42*

Ability to discriminate between different materials.   *1.51*

Stage 1 objectives

What is meant by Stage 1 is defined on page 92. Generally speaking, the children concerned will be at the beginning of the junior school.

The Unit will take a closer look at the methods, materials, tools and machinery used in building. Why bricks are laid as they are, the value of the mortar, the form and strength of frameworks, arches, buttresses, cantilevers and suspension bridges could be some of the things leading to a knowledge of the directions in which forces act and the way they balance one another.

'The wind, blowing where it listeth, pushes on my chimney pots but the chimney pots, bless them, push back at the wind just as hard, and that is why they don't fall off.'
The New Science of Strong Materials—J. E. Gordon (Pelican).

Looking at shapes will lead to experiments on strong and weak shapes, and the fact that strength depends on shape as well as on material.

Many variables are involved in bridge designing. For example, wind forces must be considered as well as the weight of the structure and the load of the traffic. There will be a great deal of model making, much for pleasure but some at least to answer questions (eg why don't the balconies fall off tall blocks of flats?), and some to experience qualities of materials or the way forces go (eg actually bridging a gap, or making a large structure from paper).

Measuring will become increasingly important in these problems. Arbitrary units of length, area, volume, weight and force will most likely be satisfactory for much of the work.

There will be a good deal of observation of structure pattern in living things and non-living things (eg birds' nests, spiders' webs, wire netting, etc).

So some objectives we could hope to achieve would be:

Interest in comparing and classifying living and non-living things.   *1.12*

Recognition of common shapes—square, circle and triangle.   *1.23*

Awareness of the structure and form of living things.   *1.26*

Recognition of the action of force.   *1.28*

Formation of the notions of horizontal and vertical.   *1.34*

Development of concepts of conservation of length and substance.   *1.35*

Awareness that more than one variable is involved in a particular change.   *1.44*

Knowledge of differences in properties between and within common groups of materials.   *1.59*

Skill in manipulating tools and materials.   *1.63*

Appreciation that properties of materials influence their use.   *1.92*

Stage 2 objectives

Stage 2 is defined on page 92. There will be no sudden change from Stage 1. The observations of structures will be more detailed (eg flying buttresses in churches, the design of motorway bridges, the balance of forces in a tower crane). The models will certainly continue. Measurement will become more accurate with the use of recognised units. The properties of materials considered will be more intangible than those which are appreciated readily by the senses (such as roughness, weight, bendability) and will involve experimental testing, for instance of the strengths of concrete or of wires.

5

There will be further observation on structure and form in living things, now more related to function and including structure visible with a good hand-lens.

The effect of structures, such as cities, or dams, on the natural balance of life ought to be dealt with.

Some objectives at this stage would be:

Preference for putting ideas to the test before accepting or rejecting them. 2.08

Awareness of internal structure in living and non-living things. 2.21

Recognition of similar and congruent shapes. 2.23

Awareness of symmetry in shapes and structures. 2.24

Ability to classify living things and non-living things in different ways. 2.25

Ability to visualise objects from different angles and the shape of cross-sections. 2.26

Development of concepts of conservation of weight, area and volume. 2.33

Ability to use representational models for investigating problems or relationships. 2.46

Familiarity with a wide range of forces and ways in which they can be changed. 2.52

Ability to measure properties of materials. 2.56

Ability to construct models as a means of recording observations. 2.74

Awareness of the impact of man's activities on other living things. 2.84

Appreciation of how the form and structure of materials relate to their function and properties. 2.92

Awareness that many factors need to be considered when choosing a material for a particular use. 2.93

Flexibility in the use of objectives

All the objectives quoted above are taken from *With objectives in mind* but it should again be stressed that there is nothing authoritarian or magical about them. They have been thought up with care and should be of help, but it would be an ideal situation if teachers would write their own, or at least some of their own. (Before doing so, please read or re-read *With objectives in mind* to be sure what objectives are about!)

From time to time, as the Unit proceeds, it is hoped that teachers will come back to look again at the objectives on these pages (or at the ones they have written themselves) to see whether any progress is being made and, in the light of what has happened, to decide what *new* objectives are dawning.

The free-flowing imaginative science work which is envisaged in this Unit implies a flexibility in the formulation and use of objectives.

In any particular teaching situation a teacher will start with a whole set of objectives in mind. Some will be general ones (eg willing participation in group work; desire to find out for oneself). These will be relevant all the time; others will be more specific.

For a particular class, a teacher will have to be aware of those children still entirely in the concrete operational stage and of those coming out of it. Particular individuals with special needs will certainly also need consideration.

On top of this, the selection of objectives will quite likely change after the activity has started. Children looking at a house under construction may be more interested in the concrete mixer than the textures of materials or 'vertical and horizontal'. The stream under a bridge or the traffic going over it may hold more important interests and experiences than thinking about compressions and tensions or the symmetry of a lattice truss. Or it may be the other way round. The art of teaching is to see these things and to be able to select and to devise the right objectives. It would be a pity to be so rigid in laying out objectives that some of the evils of the old tight syllabus were repeated. Unlike our bridges, the framework of the objectives needs to be an elastic one!

Nor should it be forgotten that teachers have objectives for their children which are almost impossible to formalise into statements. A child grows and develops under the intelligent care of a teacher in ways often difficult to translate into explicit terms and sometimes quite unforeseen. The science activities derived from the following work should contribute to this intangible but happy growth at least as much as to that development which we have been able to put in the more precise terms of our objectives.

On pages 91 to 97 will be found *Objectives for children learning science*, which is an extract from *With objectives in mind*.

London's Victoria tube line under construction. This is a cast-iron-lined running tunnel on the Highbury section of the line. It is 12ft 7in in diameter.

3 Starting points and how the work spreads out from them

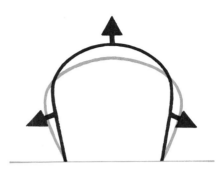

It will be better to go into this question of starting points separately and in more detail for each activity discussed later, but first, here is a story from Birmingham.

A teacher had for many years passed to school through a tunnel under a railway. One day a child happened to ask 'Why is it horse-shoe shaped?' The teacher had never thought about it, but suggested making a model to see how the forces must go when a heavy train passed over the top. Some springy metal was chosen and bent to the right shape. It had to be pegged down at the base. When a weight was placed on the top to represent a train, the top was depressed and the sides bulged outwards. Pushing the sides back held up the 'train'. It was easy to see that in a real tunnel the pushing back was done by the embankment so that there was a set of balancing forces.

But, as always, starting to answer one question showed up many more.

How do the bricks stay up?

Why was the tunnel made of bricks and not concrete?

Why are they blue bricks?

Work began on how to build arches, how to make concrete, what 'reinforcing' means, kinds of bricks and their many different properties, the history of brickmaking (from the Israelites onwards), the story of arches and tunnels, with a special look at some of the modern ones, such as the Victoria tube line and the road tunnels through the Alps.

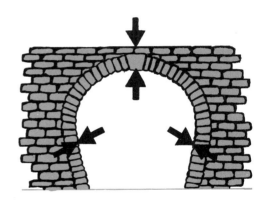

What plants and animals live on the embankment?

Why are the two sides different?

A kestrel came hunting, always on the south-facing side.

Where could it nest in a city?

What was it catching?

Everyone thought it must be catching mice, but the children searched and could find no signs of any. They did find plenty of slow-worms and were delighted to discover in a reference book that these were a favourite food of kestrels.

There is much to talk about now on the balance of living things, the effect of different conditions on life and the effect of cities. The trains themselves led to a great variety of work on speeds, destinations, goods carried, brakes, friction and air pressure.

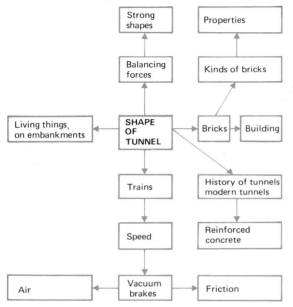

Work which developed from questioning the shape of a tunnel

The point of recording this story is to stress the importance of training ourselves, as part of our job, to look at and to ask questions about the things in our environment. We do not begin to teach science by thinking what apparatus we shall need, nor by mugging up about density or plant identification. This knowledge will almost certainly be necessary later on but the essential start is lively looking.

Starting by looking

Primary children, as yet undulled by many cares, are naturally good at looking and a beginning can often be made by taking them out and using the questions they ask. The important thing is to sort out the valuable ones; and as far as science is concerned the best are those about which some activity or experiment leading towards an answer can be devised.

Teaching didactically is of little use at a stage when children cannot learn that way. Looking, wondering, questioning and trying out come *first* not an 'introduction explaining the principles' or a 'discussion of the elements of the theory'.

We should stand and stare ourselves. Everyone seems to like to do it when a building is going up or a hole is being dug. There are many amateur experts on birds, shrubs, wild flowers or stars. Perhaps the best way to develop our own powers is to walk around with someone already skilled in observing. But look more widely than at wild flowers. The kinds of roofs on houses, the plants growing in cracks in pavements, pebbles, shells, clouds; the almost infinite variety of things can be quite fascinating. The important thing as far as science is concerned is the sort of questions we ask ourselves about the things we observe.

The environment, particularly the area immediately around a school, becomes a great source of interest and starting points. Extensive help for teachers on how to use it will be found in *Using the environment*, one of the Project's publications.

Only one point needs to be added here. The area outside the school is very important but is not the only place included in the term environment. A child of necessity, spends many hours in a classroom. This classroom environment is controlled directly by the teacher. Taking in a knobbly piece of wood, or starting a collection, perhaps of bricks, or of different textures, or of different coloured things, is *making* an environment, and if leading questions are posed and interest is focused and made active by involving the children in *doing*, then science begins. These classroom things usually come after observations outside, but sometimes may be starters.

How much should a teacher direct?

Not often can science arise absolutely casually. The teacher who did the work on the tunnel mentioned at the beginning of the chapter was very experienced, but the casual question only arose after many years. The next class was, no doubt, taken out to see, the teacher asking if the tunnel might be interesting or why the train did not push the bricks through the top. The work would not be forced along the same lines as before. The hovering kestrel might lead to bird flight, feathers and a lot about helicopters, gliders, aeroplanes and air in general, but who knows? The interest might be in the slow-worms.

What do they eat?

How do they move?

Why do they do so well in that place?

Ways of working

It will be quite obvious throughout the Unit that for much of the time children will need to work in groups. Rather than have any fixed method of arranging these, it would be better to let the nature of the work, the available material and available space dictate the number of groups working at any time and the number of children in each one. Sometimes there will be many small groups, sometimes a few large groups, sometimes large and small groups working together according to what is going on. For example, if there is a need to get a lot of results from a simple experiment, to give a reasonably good estimate of a 'correct' answer, then it might be sensible to have many pairs of children all working at the same thing. On the other hand, for visits to a building site, or on the large-scale construction of a bridge model, groups would be much bigger because of the different types of supervision required and the different materials being used.

There might even be a whole class 'production line' at times—for example, for making the paper tubes mentioned in the next chapter—but this will dissolve into small groups to make towers and domes and bridges. Then the whole lot will come together to show the results and talk about difficulties and successes, the best joints, the strongest shapes and sizes and what to do next.

For while it is obvious that a great deal of work must go on in groups, it is equally obvious that the class as a whole must come together, to draw together the threads, for the teacher to consider progress and to have a say in guiding along profitable new routes. These are key occasions and call for skill in recording and communicating.

Recording and communicating

One small intelligent six-year-old girl felt rather shy talking to visitors about what she had been doing. She simply disappeared for a few minutes and then returned to present a complete beautifully written page about it. There is more than one way of communicating.

A great variety of methods may in fact be used. Sometimes talking alone will be communication enough; one teacher wrote simply, 'I was pleased to see them discussing and helping each other.'

Drawings and paintings can be made about what was done and what was seen, pictorial ways of tabulating results and graphs of many kinds can be constructed.

Photographs and tape recordings can often be used.

Exhibitions may be set up and demonstrations may be given, perhaps for other children in the school or for parents.

Written work is very important so long as care is taken not to insist on so much of it that the exciting flow of learning is held up. There is much evidence from trial schools that the work in science has been a considerable stimulus to writing. Children who have normally been slow to write because they found it difficult have voluntarily produced a great deal more out of sheer interest, while verbally able children have poured out descriptive and imaginative work in prose and poetry.

4 An active start

Structures to make

Perhaps the most obvious way to begin is to set about constructing something simply because it is so enjoyable. Success in school depends on containing the venture within reasonable limits without being too restrictive, and a good way of doing this is by selecting materials. A few ideas follow.

Paper
What sort of structures result from sticking or pinning together flat strips of 3-cm-wide paper? Next, build another structure with similar strips but this time fold them lengthwise to form a right-angled strut. Put the two structures side by side. (There is more about shape and strength in Chapter 8.)

What could we build with sheets of newspaper? At first sight not very much seems possible with such flimsy material, but it presents a challenge similar to that faced by architects and engineers building on a larger scale.

One group began simply by pasting together sheets of newspaper until they had a beam strong enough to sit on when supported on two tables at the ends. Try it. How many sheets of newspaper does it take?

It is soon discovered that by rolling the newspaper sheets into tubes and fixing with a piece of Sellotape a useful building strut is made.

What shapes can we make?

How large a structure can we make?

Can we make one big enough to get inside?

Can we make a tower to touch the ceiling? (This might be the time to read about the Tower of Babel!)

What can we do to prevent the tower falling down so easily?

Which *shapes* are weak and which are strong?

Has symmetry anything to do with strength?

Is it best to use a few standard lengths of tube?

What is the best way to join the tubes together?

Is it the joins that are weak or the tubes?

Can we make a bridge, say, between two tables a metre apart using nothing but newspaper and Sellotape and strong enough to sit on?

'Twenty-four rolled up sheets of the *Evening Post* took over four stones. We gave up in the end because we ran out of weights. These experiments have riveted the attention of the whole class.'

Children soon discover how strong *bundles* of tubes can be.

Does the diameter of the newspaper tube make any difference to its strength?

It is interesting (if a little messy) to make tubes by pasting out sheets of newspaper with Polycell or

A bridge made from paper and glue only

similar paste and rolling the pasted sheets round a rod. If the rod is polished and the paper well soaked in paste they will slide off when wet (with a little practice). They should then be allowed to dry thoroughly.

Can we use these to make better structures?

How strong are these tubes compared with unpasted ones?

Is a *Guardian* tube stronger than an *Express* tube?

Let children devise *fair* ways of comparing the strength of tubes. The first suggestions of one class were:

Hold each end and hit it in the middle.

Get hold of it and break it.

See if we can tear it.

It may be wrong to hold up building operations too much at this point but more detailed experimental work on strength of tubes, bundles and different shapes will be found in Chapter 8.

Can you make a large geodesic dome with newspaper tubes?

(Geodesic simply means shaped like a section of the earth's surface.)

How many children can sit inside it?

The drawing shows probably the simplest design. In this all the triangles are equilateral. Some schools and playgrounds have climbing frames built to this pattern.

There are many other designs. It would be interesting to read about the architect Buckminster-Fuller who invented a lot.

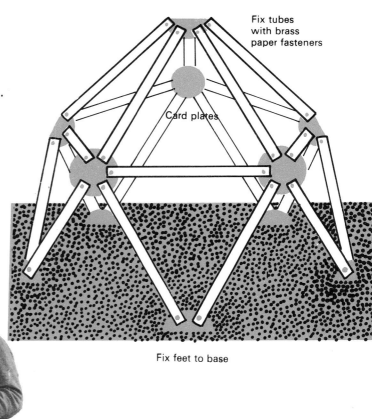

Fix tubes with brass paper fasteners

Card plates

Fix feet to base

The Minirail with the U.S. geodesic dome in the background at Expo '67, Montreal

If a dome, as shown below, is attempted, the triangles obviously cannot be equilateral, and the bases at least must reduce in size as the dome nears the top.

Are the domes strong?

What weight will each support on the top before collapsing? (You will have to fix the base of the dome to the ground.)

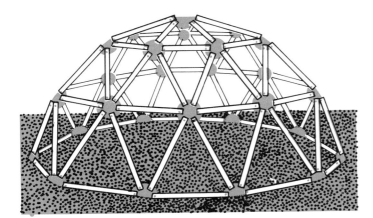

How could you find out how much the structure itself weighed? (Work out more than one way so that you can check the result. Which is the quickest way?)

Other shapes besides triangles might be tried if you can count on enthusiasm and persistence, but they are quite difficult.

One school made smaller model domes from plates cut from expanded polystyrene ceiling tiles which were either glued together or linked by loops of garden wire.

Drinking straws

The appeal of the newspaper tube structures lies in their large size and surprising strength when compared with the weak, 'floppy' starting material. Drinking straws can be used in a similar way but in this case the constructions can be built on a table. One advantage of building with straws is that experiments with joints can be made more easily. Joints between straws can be made rigid by fixing with glue, fairly rigid by using pipe cleaners or Plasticine, or free-turning by putting an ordinary pin through the straws. Engineers actually call joints like this one *pin joints*.

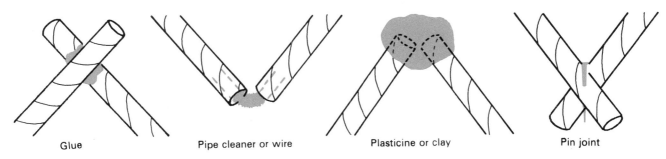

Glue   Pipe cleaner or wire   Plasticine or clay   Pin joint

Four ways of joining straws

Jumbo Jet hangar, Heathrow

Being of a standard size, drinking straws tend to produce regular mathematical models which teach a great deal; but don't neglect to try the asymmetric and even sometimes the fantastic.

An address for obtaining good quality 'art straws' is given in Chapter 12.

What is the smallest number of drinking straws you need to use to support a brick 6 cm above a table? (You are allowed to glue the straw to the brick and the table.)

Factories usually need roofs to cover the biggest possible area when supported only at the edges. Tubular structures are light and strong and are often used.

Try out some models of structures like this by glueing lengths of straw.

What is the best structure you can offer?

How are you going to decide which is *best*?

Is it the structure which, when supported at the edges, covers the largest area without sagging in the middle or is it, say, the lightest structure to cover a given area while supporting a kilogramme weight in the middle?

Poles

Bamboo poles offer an excellent material for construction on a good large scale. They are light for carrying and yet strong. Why is bamboo light and strong? Cut a garden cane across. Look at the end with a lens. The appearance may call to mind something which has already been found out about the strength of bundles. An address for obtaining large strong poles is given in Chapter 12.

Fixing together is best done by tying with sisal cord or nylon sash cord. A better grip for the cord is obtained by binding the pole with adhesive tape before lashing.

A start might be made with a wigwam, which may be made as shown in the drawing. This could lead to seeing how a modern frame tent is held up.

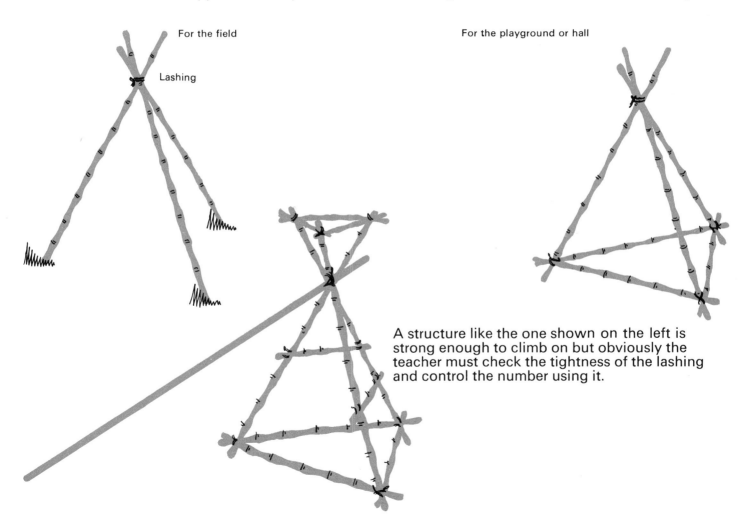

For the field

Lashing

For the playground or hall

A structure like the one shown on the left is strong enough to climb on but obviously the teacher must check the tightness of the lashing and control the number using it.

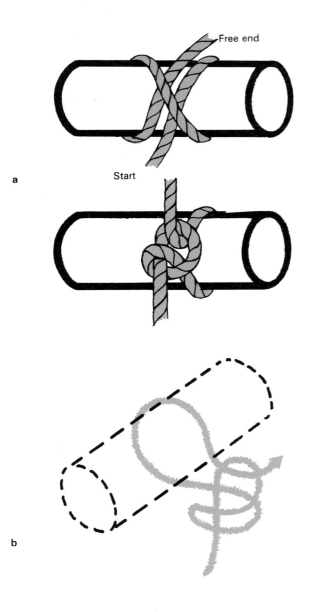

a

Free end

Start

b

To fix a cord to a pole use either (*a*) a clove-hitch or (*b*) a marlinspike.

20

A note was sent from one school : 'Some of the scouts and guides were keen to show off their skill.'

To lash two poles together start with a clove-hitch on the upright (*a*). Lash three times, bringing rope forward over the cross pole and crossing behind the upright at top and bottom (*b*) and (*c*). Cross in front of the upright and bring cord down between the poles (*d*). Then cross at the front (*e*). Bring tightly to the top and finish with a reef knot (*f*).

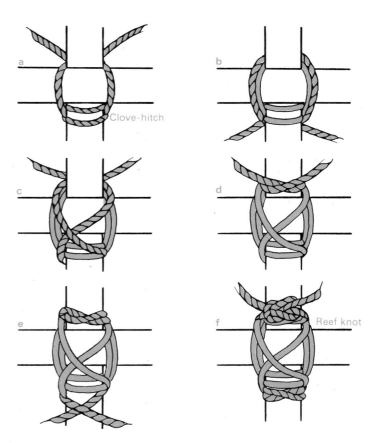

a — Clove-hitch
b
c
d
e
f — Reef knot

What other structures can be made?

One obvious use of the poles is to make bridges. This will be mentioned later. To find out what *can* be made, to find what makes for strength in a structure and to learn a proper care for safety, are the aims, rather than to give a set series of 'structures to build'.

Triangular plates

Equilateral triangles may be cut from hardboard or similar material. Sides about half a metre or a little bigger are recommended.

What can you build?

An igloo?

A space-ship?

Joining may be done simply by drilling two holes near the sides of each plate and twisting garden wire tightly through the holes.

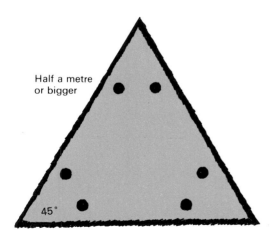

Half a metre or bigger

45°

What structures do you get by starting on different bases? Try a triangle, a square, a pentagon, a hexagon (all with sides equal to one side of the triangular plates).

The bases may be cut out of board or just marked on the floor.

What about a base with *seven* sides?

Some other materials
Blocks and timber

Some children (particularly those at Stage 1) may still enjoy building with blocks, boxes and simple structural building toys, but many will begin to find it more satisfying to use real bricks outside and to mix some mortar. Often, they can do a useful job like making the base for a garden frame, or building a wall, and this has a special appeal.

Good strong wooden boxes and manageable lengths of timber and poles are useful for huts and log cabins.

Card

Card is useful at all levels. One infant class became very interested in making boxes by drawing the 'net' on the card and then cutting and folding.

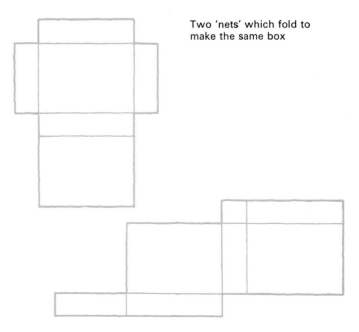

Two 'nets' which fold to make the same box

The main interest with these children was to find out how many different ways there were to do it. The challenge kept them going for several weeks at various times. Card is useful for making mathematical solids (see Nuffield Primary Maths Publications).

Balsa wood
Boys at Stage 2 enjoy making models in balsa wood, usually aeroplanes, but there are many other possibilities. A useful book is *The Solarbo Book of Models*.

Structures for pleasure

For play
One might start with climbing nets and climbing frames. Then there are Wendy houses, tree houses, play 'shelters' and tents. All are worth enjoying, building, sketching and talking about as structures. What materials are used? How are they joined? What makes them strong?

At the parks are see-saws, swings, slides, roundabouts and often nowadays some imaginative structures and sculpture to scramble on.

How do you balance heavy people against light ones on a see-saw?

Could you use one for weighing people?

What is the difference between a swing with long chains and a shorter one?

Does a heavy person swing more quickly?

Does a heavy person come down the slide more quickly?

A fairground may have a big wheel, a big dipper and many more structures.

What keeps the big dipper car going?

Does it ever go over a hill higher than the starting point?

Where is it moving fastest?... slowest?

How does the motor cyclist 'stick' to the 'wall of death'?

For aesthetic pleasure
Sculpture-structures to look at, handle and generally enjoy can be made in wood, plastic, metal or paper, and fixed with nails, bolts, clips, glue, Sellotape and so on.

Mobiles are quite fascinating and can develop in complexity. The first stage is to choose materials and invent shapes, then getting these shapes to hang in the position you want them to. Perhaps

A play structure designed and built by a grammar school for a primary school

the best way to do this is to use hooks made of thin wire to hang the shapes on to a line of string. Incidentally, a lot will be learned about centres of gravity and where to add or take away parts to balance.

Secondly, each child needs a hanging loop of string at about head height, some lengths of *thin* dowel rod, stiff wire (eg 18-swg—standard wire gauge—piano wire) or stiff plant stems (eg those of old Michaelmas daisies), some string and soft wire (or paper clips). It is easier to clip the strings to the cross beams than to tie them.

To start with, children will fix the shapes on haphazardly, getting balance by trial and error. Give them plenty of time ; soon they will want to improve and alter. The natural way seems to be to start to change at the top, but this throws all the rest out of balance. Some will find with great pleasure that the best way to build is from the bottom up. After quite a lot of experience, some, at a later stage, may like to design mobiles on paper before they start constructing them.

Exhibition structures
Some of the pavilions, built for international exhibitions, such as the Crystal Palace (1851),* the Dome of Discovery at the Festival of Britain

* Crystal Palace, alas, no longer exists, but children near London may be able to visit Bethnal Green Museum, which is constructed of cast-iron in a similar way.

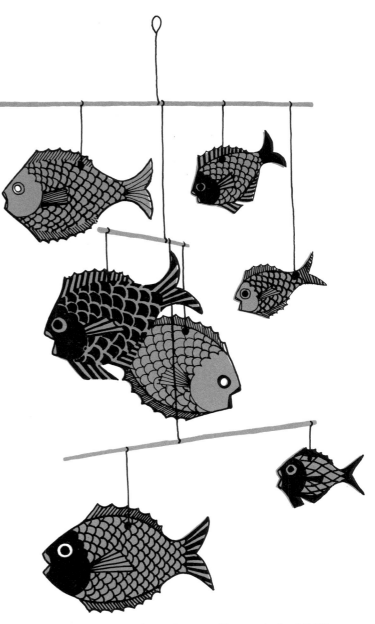

(1951) and the Atomium at Brussels in 1962, as well as being spectacular, have been experiments in structural engineering. There are many others worth looking at, even if it is only possible in pictures. Some excellent examples are

23

the Commonwealth Institute and the elephant
houses and aviary at the London Zoo.

Are they pleasant to look at ? Are they suitable for
their purpose ?

Can you design others and make models ?

A stylised tree, part of a Swiss exhibition structure

5 Looking at buildings

Another way to begin work on structures is to look at buildings. Houses, bungalows, palaces, pubs, schools, factories, churches, cinemas, swimming baths, stations, castles, garages, power stations; there is interest simply in collecting names.

What materials have been used to build these structures?

In what different ways are the building materials used?

For how many different purposes do we make buildings?

It is often possible to make regular visits to a building site. One school reported, 'The school is being extended and our work is based on the building operations. Unfortunately these are not keeping pace with the classroom work!'

Different styles of houses in the locality can be drawn, their age discovered and, no doubt, discussion will follow on how well or badly they have stood up to the weather; whether they were pleasant designs or not and what changes in such things as population and traffic have done to them. Difference in design and materials for some of the details such as windows, doors and roofs may lead into history, not only of domestic housing but of the more dramatic architecture of churches and other larger buildings.

One can with profit move out from the local examples to range through dolmens, Norman arches, Greek temples, Inca walls, St. Paul's Cathedral to Chandigarh!

The geography of houses may be considered but we should remember that igloos and mud-huts are becoming as out of date as thatched cottages.

Children at all levels have been found to be very interested in plans related to buildings they know, especially those they can see being constructed and many can make sketch plans of their own. Some like to design 'the house I would like to live in' or a building of the future, and make models from cartons, etc.

Norman arches, Durham Cathedral

Dolmen
near
Dromera

Temple
of Zeus,
Athens

Inca wall

Building designed
by Le Corbusier,
Chandigarh

According to what is available locally, one could look at particularly interesting parts of buildings, such as a hammerbeam roof (or other roof trusses), buttresses, vaulting, a dome, a spire, a cantilevered balcony or gallery.

Why was it made like that?

Where do the forces go?

Is it strong?

Often a model can be made to find some of the answers.

There follow some more direct questions and ideas about things to look for and to do.

Walls

What things are used to make walls of buildings?

What materials and designs are used for renderings or claddings?

What is used to make inside partition walls?

Do the walls carry the weight of the roof and the upper floors or do they just fill in between a load-carrying framework?

What are foundations for different kinds of walls like?

Why are they needed? (See Chapter 8.)

Simply looking at walls has led to a great variety of useful projects. One class started with the school wall and found to their amusement that some children could see over it and some not. The first result was a combined work of art, 'our class looking over the school wall', in which for each child the right amount of head had to show over the top. Starting points can be as simple as that!

Measuring heights of children and everything else

available followed. Then came an extensive piece of work on boundaries and what they were for. They were concerned about the best ways for containing different farm animals, how to get tension in wire fences and the best way to stop wooden fence posts from rotting. This involved experiments.

Why do the posts for wire fences pull over inwards on curves and corners?

What is the best way to strengthen and support these posts?

How deeply does creosote penetrate into different woods when applied in different ways?

Is it better than paint?

Is the old countryman's method of charring the ends of posts in a fire any good?

But back to walls

What plants grow on them?

Does what the wall is made of make any difference to the sort of plants?

What grows at the base of walls?

Do the same plants grow each side?

Is there any difference in your observations for a wall going north–south and one going east–west?

What animals live in walls or around their bases?

Owing to a piece of road widening outside one school, a new piece of walling had been built up to an old piece which was covered with plants growing on it.

Which would be the first to colonise the new wall?

How long would it take?

How would it be done—seeds, spores, creeping stems or rhizomes?

Could a map be kept of a piece of the new wall to show the changes?

What animals live in the old wall?

How long does it take for them to move to the new one?

Why not look at famous (and infamous) walls: Hadrian's Wall, the walls of York, the Great Wall of China, the Wailing Wall in Jerusalem, the Berlin Wall? Even acting Pyramus and Thisbe from *A Midsummer Night's Dream* might not be out of place!

How are walls built? Very often bricks are put together like this:

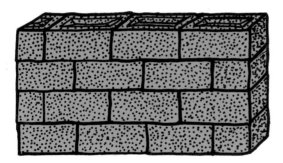

Can you compare the strength with a wall put together like this:

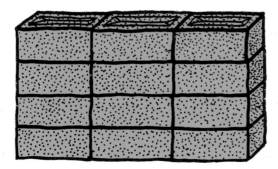

How did you do it?

Was it a fair test?

Why do you think you get the results you do?

Can you work out some more strong walls?

Look at walls to find different kinds of bonding and try them out.

Children will notice cavity walls.

What are they for? (See p. 34.)

What do the butterfly wires do?

Are cavity walls as strong as solid ones?

In some areas of the country, eg Yorkshire, Derbyshire, the Lake District, the Cotswolds, the art of dry-stone walling is still alive, methods and designs differing according to the nature of the local stone. Teachers could certainly try to let children watch it being done and perhaps try their hand.

Bricks

Can you make a collection of bricks to show in the classroom?

What are the differences?

How many different colours can you find?

What different shapes, holes and cavities are there and what are they for?

What different textures are there?

Texture patterns can be made by placing a paper over a brick and scribbling over this with a wax crayon. An alternative is to rub with a candle instead of a crayon and then wash over the paper with water colour which will 'take' where there is no wax. The idea need not be limited to bricks. One group made a good show of 'texture patterns from buildings'.

Are bricks all the same size?

Are they almost all *about* the same size?

What was the size of Roman bricks?

How do their weights vary?

Have you any bricks for special jobs such as fire bricks or engineering bricks?

What is an air-brick?

Why have them?

How many different names and marks can you find?

How are the marks put on?

Can you find where the bricks were made?

Children in one group were weighing different bricks but claimed that they couldn't do a blue engineering brick because they hadn't enough weights. They thought the answer out in the end!

The same children wondered *why* this brick was so heavy. Two guesses were made, one that it was because it had no frog (cavity) in it and the other that the 'stuff' was heavier. How can you find out which might be right?

Some other children were interested in the decay of bricks. They buried chosen kinds in soil, left some out in the open air and buried others half in and half out of the ground for a test.

Can you get some clay and try to make a brick yourself? It would dry pretty well over a radiator or in the sun, or you could bake it in an oven. Measure and weigh the brick before and after you bake it. Try to compare results from different kinds of clay. If a school has a pottery kiln, bricks could be baked in it after they have been dried.

It might be possible for some schools to arrange a visit to a brickworks and also interesting to find out something about the history of bricks.

Why could the Israelites not make bricks without straw?

Are bricks waterproof? Weigh a dry brick. Then put it in a bucket of water for a few hours and weigh again. Do different bricks give different results? (See that a blue engineering brick is included in the collection.)

Why then does the water not come through the walls of a house? Look at some cavity walls again. Why are the bricks used inside different from those used outside? Test a sample of each for soaking up water and find out the cost of each kind.

Place a soaked brick on a household balance and watch the weight as it dries. It could be recorded as a graph. Do you get the same results in different places and with different bricks? (The work may leave bricks and go on to evaporation, weather or even balances. This kind of divergence is likely throughout the Unit.)

A brick may be set up in a dish of water as shown.

Does the water rise up the brick?

How fast? (Record times and height on a graph.)

Does it rise in all bricks at the same rate?

Try to choose clean new bricks for this experiment: it is easier to see the water line.

Does the water rise at the same rate as it nears the top of the brick as it did lower down?

What could be used to stop water rising up the walls of a house from wet ground? Try any material suggested as a layer between two bricks as shown.

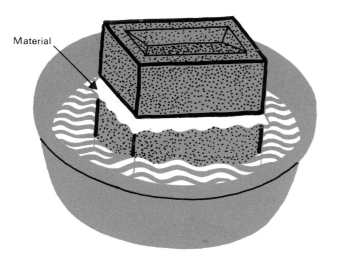

Material

One school reports that if you just place one brick on top of another the water does not rise into the second one. To do this experiment they had to mortar the bricks together as they would be in a house. It shows the need for control experiments.

What does a builder actually use?

What has been used in the past?

What happens to old buildings with no damp-proof course?

Mortar and concrete

Why do builders need piles of sand and gravel?

Where do they come from?

What is cement?

How is it made?

Why is it kept in bags?

Why is it sometimes called Portland cement?

Bricks need mortar to hold them together. Foundations, paths, balconies and lintels over doors and windows are made of concrete.

How do you make mortar and concrete?

Mortar is made by mixing cement, lime and sand in proportions 1 : 1 : 3, using just enough water to make it easy to pick up the mixture and use it with a trowel. Most classes could manage to build a small wall for the experience (even if it has to be knocked down later), but it is best to watch a bricklayer working first!

Children might watch a concrete mixer working on a site and be able to find out that, to make concrete, gravel (or stone chippings) sand and cement are mixed with water and the mixture poured out, often into a wooden mould and left to set. They may also be able to find out the proportions being used for the particular job.

The proportions, by volume, usually used are shown in the table.

	Cement	Sand	Gravel
Roofs, tunnels	1	2	3
Floors, beams	1	2	4
Foundations	1	3	5

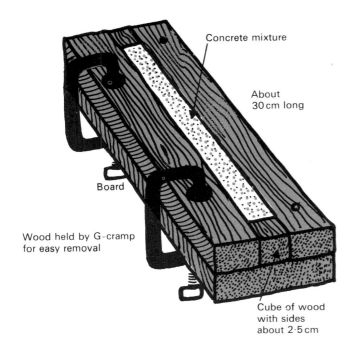

Concrete mixture

About
30 cm long

Board

Wood held by G-cramp
for easy removal

Cube of wood
with sides
about 2·5 cm

Only just enough water is used to make a stiff mixture.

Children can easily mix some concrete and make simple moulds. They can try the effect of different proportions, different kinds of chippings in place of gravel and the difference if a sloppy mixture is made instead of a stiff one.

If a mould similar to the one shown is constructed, standard-sized bars about 30 × 2.5 × 2.5 cm can be cast on which tests of strength can be made. Grease the inside surfaces a little and fill the mould level with the top with mixtures with differing proportions of cement, sand and gravel (use a cup or similar measure). Several exactly similar moulds will shorten the time taken. Several blocks are needed from each mix to make sure that results are repeatable.

The drawing shows one way of testing the strength of the bars. There are many others.

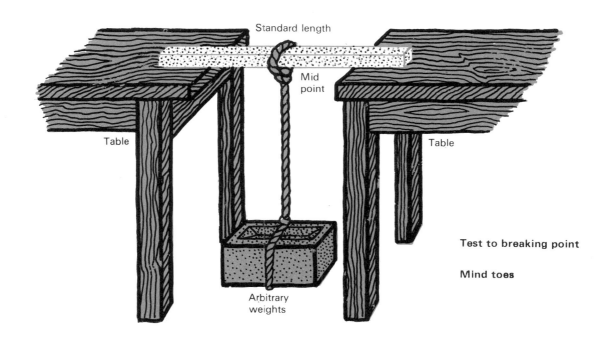

Standard length

Mid
point

Table

Table

Arbitrary
weights

Test to breaking point

Mind toes

Ways of recording graphically should be used.

What is the effect of including a knitting needle or wire in the mould for reinforcing ? Can reinforcing be seen on the site ?

Children are also often interested in devising an impact test. A differently shaped block is needed. One group made blocks by casting them in plastic drinking cups using cement to sand in the proportions 1 : 1, 1 : 2, 2 : 1, 4 : 1, 6 : 1, 8 : 1. They soon learned the importance of good labelling, and did it well. How should the test be made ? Hitting the blocks with a hammer was the favourite suggestion, but Richard wouldn't allow this, claiming that *he* would hit it a lot harder than Sandra. No one wanted to give either Richard or Sandra the pleasure of hitting them all, even if they did try to be fair every time, and so it was decided to drop an iron weight on to the block, always from the same height and to count the number of drops needed to smash the concrete. Other children have decided to drop a standard weight, steadily increasing the height of the drop until the block breaks and recording the heights needed to break the different concrete mixes on a graph.

Keeping the rain out

Look at the roofs in your district. How many different designs are there ? Look for pitched roofs, flat roofs, domes, spires, etc. There may even be some modern curved roofs of the hyperboloid type.

How does the pitch vary ? Does it change according to when the house was built ? Look for 'hipped' roofs, gables, dormer windows set in the roof, decorated barge boards and finials.

Dormer window

Finial

Barge-board

Hipped roof

How many different ways of making a *flat* roof can you find?

What covering materials are used for roofs?

How many kinds of tiles are there?

How are they fixed on?

What sizes and colours of tiles are made?

What are they made of?

Collect examples.

How do pantiles fit together?

What are slates?

What does thatch come from?

How thick does it have to be?

Does it last?

Where in the country are flat stones used for roofs?

What are the advantages of cedar-wood tiles?

Bitumen-impregnated felt is used under tiles and also in several layers for a finished roof and one may also find corrugated iron, corrugated plastic and metal sheets (aluminium, copper and, particularly on church roofs, lead. See the Unit *Metals, Stages 1 & 2* or *Background*).

It is interesting to compare thickness and weights of these materials. How is flashing fixed so that rain does not run between a roof and a wall?

What is the timber roof structure like under tiles?

A real building may be observed and a model made. What support do other kinds of roof need? (A covered court at Wimbledon has a dome of concrete 76 mm [3 in] thick. Its span is 53 m [175 ft] and it is only supported at the four corners.)

How does rain get away from roofs? Look at guttering and fall pipes. They may be made of wood, iron or plastic and this may lead to work on rotting and rusting and their prevention. Old houses sometimes have fall pipes cast in lead with dated decorations.

It would be interesting to look at gargoyles on churches. Another sideline would be drains and sewage disposal.

Keeping a house warm

While talking about roofs, insulation of glass fibre or exfoliated vermiculite chips might be mentioned and lead to the topic of keeping a house warm.

An experiment might be set up as shown, to compare the heat-insulating qualities of different materials.

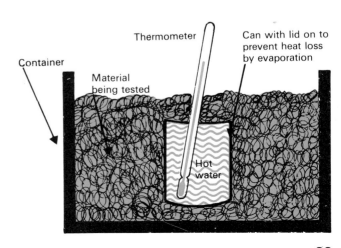

Container

Thermometer

Can with lid on to prevent heat loss by evaporation

Material being tested

Hot water

Materials sold for insulating pipes, tanks, walls and ceilings may be compared and wood shavings, cotton wool, screwed-up newspaper, etc, may be tried.

To compare the heat-insulating properties of bricks, breeze blocks, Thermalite block, wood, etc, it is possible to use the material to form a little cavity to put the can of hot water in. Make the cavity as tight fitting as possible.

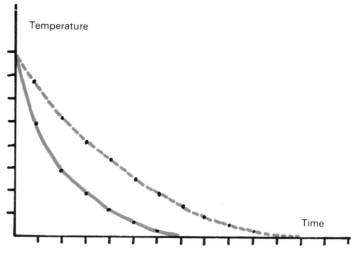

Children may see that 'the steeper the graph, the quicker it is cooling'.

Does the cavity in the walls help to keep the house warm (ie is air a good heat insulator)?

An experiment like the one shown can be tried.

You would have to see that there was the same amount of test material around the can each time to be fair. The easiest way would be to use equal-sized building blocks.

Start with water at the same temperature each time.

You can then either simply see how much the hot water cools in an hour for the different packings you try, or, better, plot a cooling curve by noting the temperature every fifteen minutes.

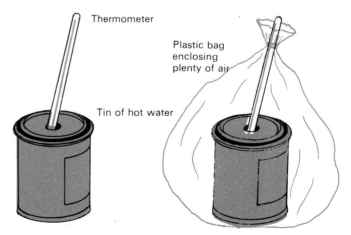

Which one cools down quicker?

How can you show that any effect is not all due to the plastic bag?

Isn't there air round the tin on the left anyway?

Why shouldn't this insulate as well as the other?

How many ways are there of heating a house?

What is the difference between convector and radiator heaters?

(This may lead off to work on heat and temperature, electricity, gas, oil and coal, smokeless zones, etc.)

More materials used in building

Wood
What kinds and what sizes are commonly used?

Look at roof timbers, floors (boards and blocks), skirting, doors, door and window frames, partitions, timber cladding for outside walls and scaffolding planks.

What man-made timber is used? (Hardboard, blockboard, chipboard, plywood.) How are they made? A great deal more detail will be found in the Project's Unit, *Working with Wood, Background information*.

Metals
Again there is a complete Unit on metals, so only a short reference will be made here.

Look for the steel girder frameworks of large buildings, the shapes of the girders and how they are fixed (see Chapter 8).

Scaffolding might lead to a study of frameworks, strength of tubes, rusting and galvanising (covering with a coat of zinc to prevent rusting). A zinc coating is also used on the cold-water tanks in a house, although the latest ones are of glass fibre or polypropylene.

Aluminium is used for window frames, fittings like door handles and sometimes in sheet form on roofs or as cladding for walls.

Copper is sometimes used as a roof cover, especially on domes. It weathers to a beautiful green colour because a layer of copper salts is formed.* This might lead to some chemistry. The main use of copper is in pipes, the hot-water cylinder and electric wires. Some children might be interested in hot-water systems and house wiring.

Lead is still used in 'flashing', and the cold-water pipes of old buildings will be of lead though it is hardly ever used now. Can you find out why it was not used for hot-water pipes?

Cast-iron is used for guttering, rain-water pipes and inspection cover lids.

Plastics
Plastics are being used more and more for buildings and some of the plumbing in the house is now done with plastic pipes. Other uses are for floor coverings, gutters and rain-water pipes, electrical fittings, other fittings like door catches and bell pushes, and for tiling ceilings and walls.

The Project has a Unit *Children and plastics.*

Other materials
Glass, putty, paint, glue, glazed drainpipes, asbestos sheet, plaster and plaster-board all need looking at and discussing if only to consider how they are made.

Children are often quite puzzled about what glass is and some nine-year-olds were very interested to find that the roof of the school kitchen was made of asbestos. They had never heard of it.

---

* *In the country it would be a layer of copper carbonate; in towns it would more likely be of basic sulphate; and by the sea of basic chloride.*

Fitting and fixing things

A collection and exhibition of *things for building* is well worth making. It could include a section on *fixing things for a house* (all the shapes and sizes of nails, screws, bolts, rivets, shelf brackets, wall plugs, glues, etc).

Tools and machines for building

When investigating building operations, children's first interest is very often the machinery: the concrete mixers, bulldozers, trench diggers, tipping lorries and cranes. They like to draw them and to make models. The models will vary in sophistication according to the stage of development of the children, younger ones working very simply with card, boxes and scrap material, while older ones will concentrate on *working* models, bringing into the work wood, metal and structural toys like Meccano.

A good idea is to look for ways of lifting heavy weights. No doubt there will be a slope, a wheelbarrow, a pulley. These can be tried out in school. A box of books too heavy to be lifted on to a table can quite easily be wheeled up a slope or even pushed up without wheels. A strong piece of timber can be used as a crowbar to lift up the same heavy box. With a builder's plank and a strong low support a small child can lift the teacher off the ground.

The experiences that a child gains from a wooden lever of various lengths gives him valuable experience through his own senses of what later he may deal with mathematically. There are more details in Chapter 8.

Use a *plumbline* and *spirit level*. These are quite cheap to buy and easy to make. A plumbline is simply a weight on a string. Quite a good spirit level can be made as shown. Tubing 10–15 mm diameter works well and the level may be 30–40

cm long. It helps to put just one spot of washing-up liquid in the water.

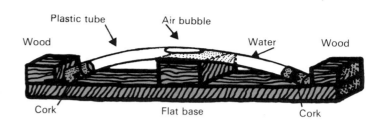

Let the children try out a large number of things. (It is surprising how many walls, floors, tables, etc, are out of true.) The meaning of the words *vertical* and *horizontal* quickly become clear.

The use of a *square* follows easily and the idea of a *right angle*. Children may use the carpenter's try-square for testing the 'squareness of things'

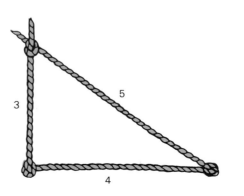

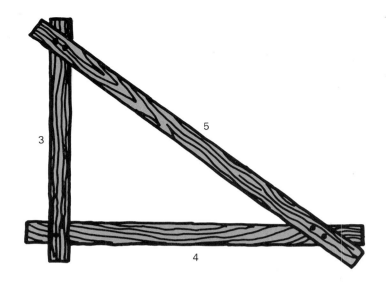

and also make the famous 3.4.5. triangle, either with knotted string or pieces of wood.

These triangles could be used to lay out a plan on the playground or field and mention made of how clever the early Egyptians were when they set out the pyramids.

Are all *trowels* the same shape? Compare the bricklayer's trowel with a gardener's trowel and plasterer's float.

Has the shape anything to do with the use?

Why does a bricklayer's trowel have a point?

Why is the handle set higher than the blade?

What factors decide how big a trowel is used?

The only way to find out is to mix some mortar and try using it to put a few bricks together.

Other lines arising from observations of buildings

Pipes
How many different kinds of pipes are used when houses are built?

What are they all for?

What different materials are they made of?

What different sizes are they?

How are they fitted together?

How are they made to go round corners?

Observations, collecting specimens and measuring may lead to many pieces of work. One might be on water supply, including rainfall and reservoirs and the hot and cold-water systems of houses—while not forgetting to calculate how much water we each use per day and to consider the general world water shortage situation. Some teachers might wish to branch off here on a wider study of water and its properties.

Another line of work, perhaps starting from looking into a waste-water inspection chamber, could be about sewage disposal. This could involve ideas from simply observing the need for fall in drains to studying methods of separation, bacteria, life cycles and food chains. Again the local and world-wide problems of disposal of waste are important matters to discuss, not forgetting the health problems which still arise in many places in the world from the complete absence of any method at all for the disposal of sewage.

The slow history of development in this country is quite revealing and children could be taken to look at fresh rivers near their sources and then follow what happens to them as they make their way to the sea in order to see some of the present unsolved problems.

37

Wires
What kind of wires are used in a house?

How do they go?

One could look at switches, meters, junction boxes and fittings and move to some elementary work on electricity.

The animals and plants connected with a house
Teachers interested are recommended to read *The Living House*, by Ordish (Hart Davis).

One expert on spiders used to startle his audience by saying that however particular they were he would guarantee that he could find at least three species of spider in their houses! Apart from spiders we might consider flies, clothes moths, other moths which fly to lights, harvestmen, earwigs, woodlice, carpet beetles, woodboring beetles, mice and all the pets people keep.

As for plants, one could look at dry rot and the conditions in which it flourishes, other fungal growths on food and leather, mosses and lichens, house plants and garden plants.

Some mathematics
How many bricks does it take to build a house? A builder might give a clue.

How could you count them? The good maths thinking here is that

a. We cannot get an exact answer so we have to agree about the degree of accuracy we will accept.

b. There is no answer in the book so we have to devise means of checking, probably by getting someone to do it independently, but even better by devising more than one method of counting.

About how much would all the bricks weigh?

Could you find out how much a whole house weighs? (What about the need for foundations?)

How many trees would it need for the timber (including fences)?

How much water does an ordinary household use in a day?

How much water does a school use in a day?

How much water does an electric power station (or a local factory) use in a day?

Can you calculate how much rain falls on the school playground—say, in a month?

Other sidelines arising
There are so many other valuable ways in which to let the work flow arising from the particular situation. A teacher is soon aware of these.

Some children, looking at buildings, found a 300–400 year-old thatched cottage with a wood frame structure and an iron tie-bar holding up a bulging wall.

There was enough science here, the teacher was pleased to see, for a long time—roofing, rigid frameworks, expansion of metals and strength of materials—but at that moment the dear old lady who lived in the cottage invited them all inside to show her treasures, her bedroom, her kitchen, her oven. Science became sociology for a time. Did it matter?

6 Looking at bridges

The Mekong River is 2,600 miles long and in its whole length there is not a single bridge. The situation in Britain is very different. We have bridges galore, many examples can be found and within a short distance of almost any school. These bridges carry footpaths, farm tracks, roads, railways, rivers and canals over each other and are of many ages, sizes and methods of construction.

The Severn suspension bridge

'The Mathematical Bridge', Queen's College, Cambridge

Spectacular bridges make an obvious interest for some areas ; the Thames bridges in London, the Clifton and Severn suspension bridges and the swing bridges in Bristol, the Tyne bridges, the Scottish bridges over the Forth and Tay and the Menai Strait bridges are some examples. But not all spectacular bridges are large ones. Those at Cambridge, the iron bridge at Coalbrookdale, a packhorse bridge in Derbyshire or the clapper bridge on Dartmoor are equally exciting, while for delicate elegance some of the footbridges over our motorways could hardly be beaten.

In practice, the best start for most schools is to see what bridges exist in the immediate locality. It is quite a surprise for many to carry out a survey of *bridges near our school* and to find the number and variety within a mile or so.

How are they made ?

What materials are used and what type of structure is it ?

What is their purpose ?

How much are they used ?

What sort of traffic uses them and at what time of day is the traffic heaviest ?

When were they built ?

Have the needs changed since then ?

Are they good enough now ?

Have they been altered ?

Out of the observation will come drawings, sketch maps and models. To make the models a good deal of measurement and an idea of scale will be needed. The use of Ordnance Survey maps may develop.

One school, situated on a fairly short river, looked at all bridges which spanned it from the source downwards. Another, mainly from a coach, did a sketch and photograph survey of the bridges over a length of motorway.

Models

Looking at bridges almost always leads to model making. Models are enjoyable to make and look good but a good deal of thought should be given to other reasons why they are being made. It is all very well to make something which looks like the real bridge, and maybe that is as far as the earliest primary children want to be taken, but soon there should be attention to getting the scale right and more especially to getting forces right, ie making the structure of the model *work* the same way as the original. These are models which can be used for testing and can be built in such a way as to show up some of the engineering problems involved.

The story of a ten-year-old boy illustrates the point well. He made a model of the Severn bridge which looked like the bridge shown below.

He was disappointed because it did not look right. The teacher initiated a lot of discussion about this and it was decided that the scale must be all wrong and that this model was not a suspension bridge anyway because the roadway would stand up without any strings. Then there were parts missing from each end.

Actual dimensions were looked up in the library:

The main span is 3240 ft [955 m] with two side spans of 1000 ft [300 m]. The towers are 400 ft [122 m] high and the legs are not solid, but are cellular, made from tubes of steel plate from 1 in [25.4 mm] to $\frac{9}{16}$ in [14.3 mm] thick.

When he began to model to scale, the boy was astonished. To go on to his classroom table, the towers had to be just 3 in [76 mm] high. The roadway would have to be of thin paper and the suspension would certainly have some work to do.

In the real bridge the cables are 20 in [508 mm] diameter and are made from 8322 wires of $\frac{1}{5}$ in. [5.08 mm] diameter. The main cables for the

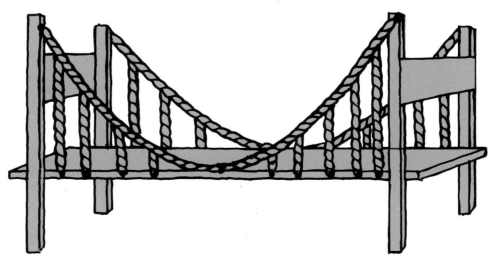

model would need to be only a little more than $\frac{1}{100}$ in [0·254 mm] in diameter. Linen thread was the nearest that could be managed. The roadway was not flat but was distinctly arched.

The model looked something like this:

Quite a large group was becoming interested and other models were looked at more critically.

The need to anchor the ends of the suspension wires became obvious when loads were tried and the towers leaned inwards. Figures for the real bridge were found again.

Pull on anchorages = 20 000 tons force.
Load at top of towers = 6600 tons force from each cable.

The balance of forces in a suspension bridge was realised.

compression and *tension* when the difference is seen between how the forces go in the cables.

The actual value of models in real bridge construction should be mentioned. Even with accurate calculations, scale models are usually carefully tested. Telford made a large model of his Menai bridge before he dared to build the real one, and model sections of the roadway of the Severn bridge were tested in wind tunnel experiments, resulting in a unique design, not only of the sections themselves but of the method of suspension.*

The trouble with *small* models is that the actual problems involved in bridging a large gap do not arise. For example, you always have material long enough to go right across, and power and reach to put any part of the structure in any position— even to lift the whole thing up. A bridge builder

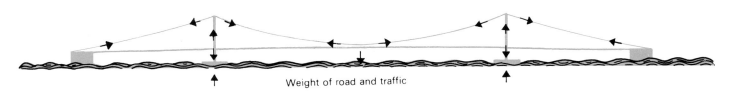

Weight of road and traffic

The forces in a suspension bridge balance each other

A start may now be made on the fundamental realisation that forces always come in pairs; where there are forces there are always others in the opposite direction to balance them (as long as nothing moves). Try to describe these forces: the tension force in the cable to hold up the road; the push of the tower to hold up the cable; the push of the other end of the tower on the earth; the push of the earth against the foot of the tower.

A beginning may also be made on the ideas of

is faced with the problem of crossing a large gap, often without the chance of supports in the middle, having only short lengths of material or thin wires to build with and all the difficulties of getting men, machines and materials to the other side.

Children ought to 'feel' this problem of a bridge.

See 'Aerodynamic Studies for the Severn Bridge', Project No. 6.

One teacher carefully placed all the tables in her room in two rows wide apart one morning and told her eight-year-olds that they were not going out to play until at least one of them had got from one row to the other without touching the floor, using materials which were about the school. The smallest girl just managed it in time (a few inches above the floor) with the help of some PE ropes.

The whole class was galvanised! All the bridges in the district were inspected with much appreciation of the problems. The head produced an aerial photograph and science and local geography flourished.

No one should underestimate the amount of thought and preparation behind such work. The teacher in question had taken some time planning the idea and had surveyed for herself the structural material which was available. She had estimated that the job was within the children's ability and had several ways in her mind for helping out if necessary. Success is important to eight-year-olds.

Much can be learnt from attempting to experience the engineering difficulties by working on a larger scale outside. You find that you can build towers for a suspension bridge on the two banks, but how are you going to get the first line across? It is said that a bow and arrow were used to carry the first line over the River Avon for the Clifton bridge.

A wide strip representing a river might be marked on a playing field and an attempt made to construct a suspension bridge with poles, planks and rope. Several schools have used PE equipment successfully.

Obviously there are precautions to take:

1. Work on turf and *not* on a hard playground or indoors, where constructions will slip. On turf, poles and large tent pegs can be knocked in firmly.

2. Any decking which children walk over should be very near to the ground so that any failures in the structure can let anyone fall only a few inches.

3. For suspension bridges see that the lines each side of the uprights make equal angles as shown.

In this way the resultant forces will only tend to force the uprights more firmly into the ground. Unequal angles will tend to pull them over.

Types of bridges

So far we have considered only the suspension bridge. Some other common types and models which may be made are now discussed. There are many variations and these should be looked for locally and in pictures. The factors which make for a good-looking bridge ought to be considered, and much help will be found for this in the HMSO booklet *The Appearance of Bridges*, which has many illustrations.

Single-beam bridges
The first bridges in Britain of any size and permanence were made of monolithic stone slabs supported at their ends.

Simple plank bridges are useful to cross small distances. One can be made using a builder's plank or PE equipment (floorboarding is *not* strong enough).

The amount of sag may be measured when

different children stand in the middle and a graph made of sag against weight.

What difference does it make if heavy weights are placed on the ends of the plank ?

Cantilever bridges

Historically, these may have been the next bridges to appear, possibly in China, where stones were built outwards in this manner.

A model should be tried. How much does the strength of this bridge depend on the weight of the abutments ?

The next drawing shows the very simplest model of a cantilever bridge.

The Forth railway bridge is a much more complex version.

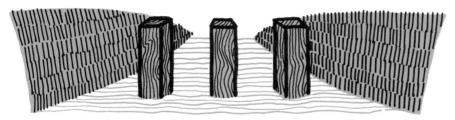

An interesting activity is to construct a model bridge in the same way that the Forth bridge had to be made, starting with towers, then building out each side keeping a balance and finally pushing out a girder or beam to close the gaps.

The following sketches show models of cantilever
bridges which might be cut from plywood,
hardboard or thick card. The importance of the
downward thrust on the ends of the bridge will
soon be noticed.

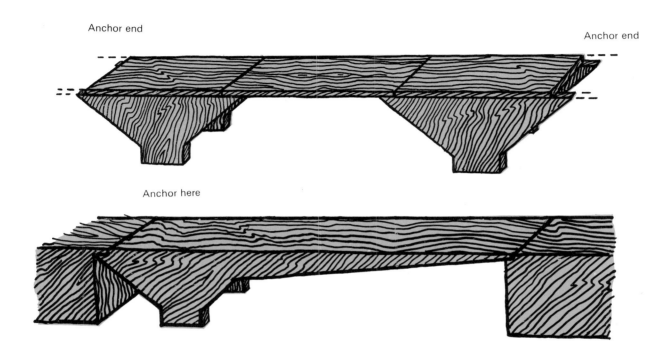

Anchor end

Anchor end

Anchor here

Arch bridges

The oldest surviving arch bridge dates from the
ninth century BC and stands at Smyrna in Turkey.
Teachers might like to work on the history of
bridges, looking at, for example, Roman bridges,
medieval bridges, Florentine bridges, the story of
London Bridge, the iron bridge at Coalbrookdale.
There is much of interest in the biography of
famous bridge builders, for example, Brunel,
Telford, Rennie, John Wilkinson and Abraham
Darby. The book *Bridges and Men* listed in the
bibliography will help.

Models of arch bridges may be made either with flexible balsa sheet or Meccano strip, supporting the roadway above the arch or suspending it below.

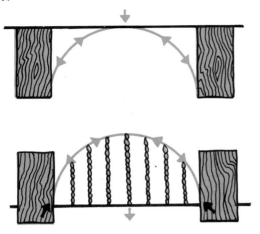

The need for some means of pushing back against the outward thrust of the arch is soon discovered. Abutments for arch bridges must be big and heavy.

It is interesting to make a model of a stone arch bridge with wedge-shaped blocks made from clay or cut from wood. A former made from half a can or a bent piece of card, plastics, etc, is used to build the arch on and removed when it is finished.

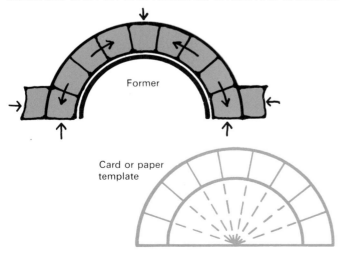

Former

Card or paper template

A card template made as shown helps to get the right shape for the blocks. With small models the 'stones' may have to be glued together. A good large model can be made by cutting shaped blocks of expanded polystyrene. Large blocks of this material 10—15 cm thick can be obtained from builders' merchants. The easiest way to cut this has been found to be by gently sawing with a long hacksaw blade (use the blade alone). Experiments should be made altering the sizes and number of the blocks forming the arch. Why should it always be an odd number?

There are some very graceful modern arch bridges, often with slender shallow arches of pre-stressed reinforced concrete.

An interesting arch structure used for motorway footbridges and for frameworks for large factory buildings is the three-pin arch.

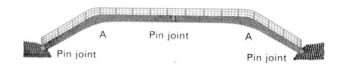

A   Pin joint   A
Pin joint   Pin joint

It makes a good model.

What are its advantages?

How does it compare with a single arch of the same size?

Is there any reason for making the bridge thicker at A?

Truss bridges
These developed from the need to lengthen the span of simple plank bridges. Models may be constructed from balsa wood strip or drinking straws.

A simple truss which was used as long ago as the thirteenth century is shown in the drawing.

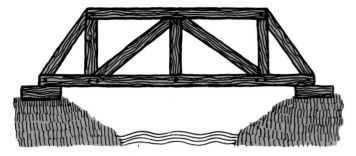

Truss bridges were used a great deal for timber railway bridges in the rapid expansion of America. They were often very badly constructed.

We can often see iron bridges with a *lattice truss*.

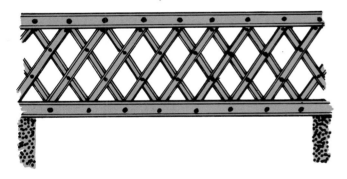

There are also *trussed arches* like the Sydney Harbour bridge or, in this country, the Runcorn–Widnes bridge.

Other kinds of bridges
There are many other types, for example the bridle-chord bridge over the River Wye. This bridge comes immediately after the Severn suspension bridge on the M4 motorway.

Bridges which move could be an interest and some children might attempt working models of swing bridges, lift bridges, transporter bridges or bascule bridges (eg Tower Bridge in London) especially if these can be seen locally.

The Wye bridge—an example of a bridle-chord bridge

Teachers will hardly need reminding of the opportunities for doing some world geography too, not only finding out where famous bridges are but wondering why they are there.

Why aren't there any bridges over the Mekong?

A sad but important study could be about bridges which fell down, the timber bridge of the US railroads already mentioned, the Tay Bridge disaster of 1879 (William McGonagall's verses would be appreciated!), the Tacoma Narrows in 1940 (see Chapter 12 for details of a film loop) and the disasters to box-girder bridges at Milford Haven and Melbourne in 1971 might be examples used.

7 More structures worth looking at

There is a multitude of other worth-while structures to look at, to ask similar questions about and to make models of. One might be a rotary clothes drier.

What materials are used?

Why is it made of tubes?

Is it a strong shape?

Where do the forces go?

Which are pulls and which are pushes?

How does the push upwards of the earth balance the weight of the clothes?

Or it could be a harp or the frame of a piano which carries the strings (a sideline from work on sound perhaps); or it could be tents.

What different kinds of tents are there?

How are they kept up?

How do the forces go in guy-ropes and in the frames?

Towers

Church towers and spires, like the tower of Babel mentioned earlier, have often fallen down, not as a punishment to their builders for aspiring too near to heaven, but because they were put up by rule of thumb. Their builders didn't realise how big the forces were, along what line the forces went, or even what were the strengths of the materials they were using. It is interesting to collect records of the collapse of church towers. Often the foundations were simply not good enough for the weight. What *is* the weight of a church tower?

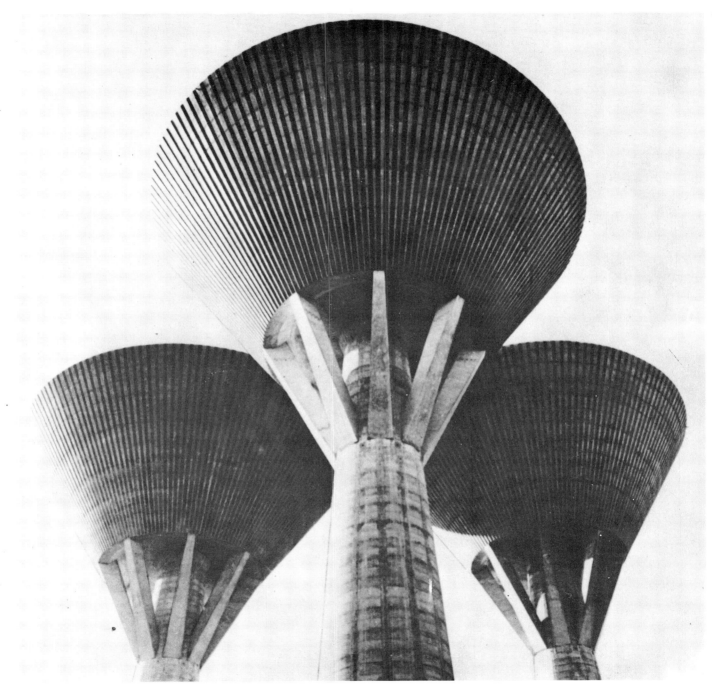

Water towers at Alencon

More commonly the weight of the roof and the thrust outwards of the arches pushed out the walls. All was well with wooden roofs of the pattern shown.

Buttresses were used for strengthening walls to counterbalance the outward thrust (in towers, usually at the corners). It is worth looking at towers and buttresses and sketching the direction of the forces.

They were not very heavy and, having a tie beam, there was no sideways push, but when roofs were made of stone vaulting the outwards push was considerable.

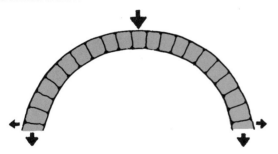

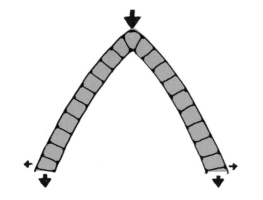

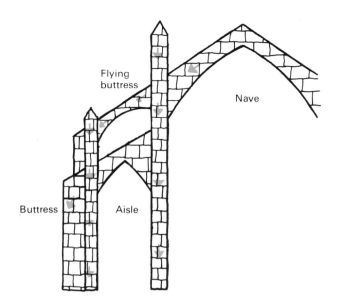

Inverted arch at Wells Cathedral

This pushing outwards of walls often happens in houses, farm buildings and old warehouses. In these cases the walls were usually pulled together by iron bars across the whole building with S or X-shaped supports on the outside. These can often still be seen.

The outward thrust of the dome of St Paul's Cathedral is matched by the inward pull of a steel chain around the base.

At Wells Cathedral the builders made a mistake the opposite way round from usual. They made the walls push inwards too hard and had to put in the famous inverted arches to compensate.

The tower at Pisa is one that did not *quite* fall down. Why did this one survive? It can be used to introduce the stories of Galileo (and thence perhaps gravity, pendulums and telescopes).

The steel girder construction of the Eiffel and the Blackpool towers make a good contrast with the modern Post Office tower, where all the rooms and galleries are built round a strong reinforced-concrete tube.

TV and radio masts are also spectacular structures, older ones being built of steel lattice girders often balanced on a pivot at the base and held vertically by steel guy-ropes to take the wind strain. Newer masts are slim tubes and go up to about 300 m [1000 ft]. (Some children might like to tackle the practical problem of making a fishing-rod or other flexible tall rod stand vertically and firmly.)

Electricity pylons and the cooling towers at generating stations might lead to work on electricity, condensation, turbines and energy as well as on structure. Why should cooling towers be the shape they are? The walls are quite thin (100–250 mm). Apart from economy and lightness how does this help?

A number of TV masts and cooling towers have collapsed. We have not done so much better than the church tower builders! It has usually been wind forces and extra weight due to ice formation which have not been estimated correctly.

Other towers to look at are those for the floodlights on football grounds, and even lamp-posts. The old-fashioned lamp-posts are simply strong iron tubes, but modern ones are in pre-stressed concrete. Lamp-posts in simple concrete would be heavy and clumsy looking and would snap quite easily so steel wires are placed inside the concrete mixture and kept under tension while it sets. Then the posts can be made slender and they even bend quite gracefully in a strong wind.

Look out for cast-iron lamp-posts which have a bracket support for an arm underneath and for steel lamp-posts in which the support for the arm will be from above. This is because cast-iron is stronger in compression, while steel is strong in tension.

Cranes

Most children can watch various types of cranes working. In cities particularly, the tower crane used in building high blocks of flats will be common.

How many different types of crane can be found?

How is the structure made light but rigid?

How are load and the long arm balanced on the other side?

How many different movements can a crane make?

How is the tower crane made taller when it is needed?

How do the forces go?

Models are popular. They should be refined as far as the children's ability will allow.

A competition could be held to construct the strongest and lightest beam for a model crane. How could the competition be made fair? It will need discussing. Perhaps the best way is to decide on the length of the beam (say 50 cm) and material to be used, eg, balsa strip of a certain size or drinking straws. Then with one end fixed, weights can be hung on the other end until the beam breaks. This breaking weight should be recorded as a multiple of the weight of the beam itself.

Ships

Some secondary schools build canoes or dinghies. Most children can make model boats. How is a strong framework built up? Is the same method used for large ships? (Most schools will have to rely on photographs of ship-building yards.)

The forces acting on a sailing boat are quite complicated and it would probably be sufficient at this stage to see how sails can be adjusted to make the boat sail with the wind or against it, either by watching boats or by experimenting with models. (A steady wind indoors can be made with a vacuum cleaner.) It would be interesting to see how shape and structure of boats has changed over the centuries. Work on floating and sinking may arise. There is a discussion on the forces on boats in the Unit *Science from toys, Stages 1 & 2*.

Roads

One of the best starts is to watch road building in progress.

How many different materials are used?

How are kerbs fixed?

What is tarmac?

Where does tar come from?

Why is a road not made exactly level?

What is banking on a curve for?

Where does the water go when it drains down the gutter?

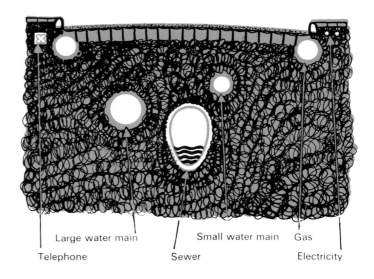

Large water main   Small water main   Gas

Telephone   Sewer   Electricity

This section of a road shows the services running under it

What are all the pipes and wires which run under roadways?

Take advantage of every opportunity to look at holes dug in the road.

Some teachers might like to follow up; electricity supply, water supply, sewerage, telephones. A sideline would be road safety including speed, friction and skidding, road signs and how well the different lettering and colour contrasts used for them can be seen. History is relevant in such questions as:

How did the Romans make such good roads?

Who was Macadam?

Tunnels

More and more underground structures involving tunnels are being made to relieve traffic congestion. Perhaps the most complicated one in the world is the London Underground Railway system. We haven't any road tunnels to compare with the spectacular ones bored through the Alps, but the stories of how these were made and of the remarkable efforts to build the early railway tunnels in Britain before much power machinery was available, are worth telling.

Dams

Some schools will be able to visit dams, probably in connection with a study of water supply.

What shape do they have to be made? Why are they so much wider at the bottom than the top?

What are the pressures like in deep water? A well-known experiment is shown.

Drill the holes in the container exactly the same size. Use sticking plaster to cover them (not

Sellotape). Peel off just one piece of plaster each time. Keep the water-level in the can constant, ie fill up to a mark after each test. How does the pressure change with depth?

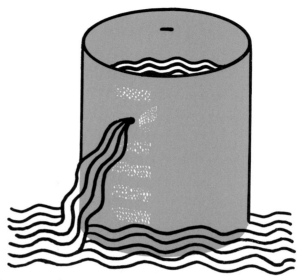

Do not miss talking about the dams at Aswan, Kariba and Tennessee Valley. This will almost certainly lead to discussion on conservation which could be taken further, especially looking at local events such as the removal of hedges and trees. By sprinkling water on two sloping seed boxes of

Trevallyn dam, Tasmania

54

soil, one with turf over the soil and one without, it is easy to see what happens when vegetation cover is destroyed.

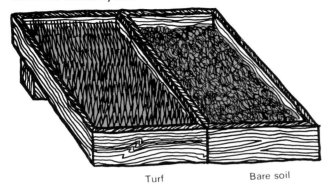

Turf   Bare soil

Other ideas

The following additional starting-point suggestions might also be useful:

Railway stations St Pancras train shed made engineering history.

Drilling rigs For North Sea gas for example. (Perhaps gasholder would follow?).

Furniture What joints and fixings are used and how is it designed to keep it rigid?

Telescopes The radio telescopes, for example at Jodrell Bank, at Parkes in Australia or at Nancay in France are remarkable structures and it might be worth looking at pictures of the structure Herschel rigged up for his optical telescope and of the mechanism at Mount Palomar.

North Sea drilling rig

The Jodrell Bank radio telescope

8 Some Investigations

The experimental work outlined here will no doubt be used by teachers in many different ways, but at best it is set up to try to answer questions which have arisen from observations such as those suggested earlier. It is never satisfactory to do an experiment only once or to leave it without comparing with others and discussing with them.

An experiment should not be set up to demonstrate a preconceived answer but in order to find out. Of course, the teacher has an objective and knows what is *likely* to happen, but in most cases (by asking the right question usually) the activity can be one of satisfying discovery for the children.

There are times when (from the teacher's point of view) the experiment 'doesn't work'. These often lead to most rewarding investigations. For example a group were trying out the strength of box girders and made some about 5 cm square from card.

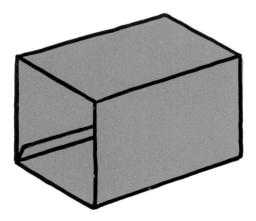

Box girder made from card

They were found to have little strength and flopped over when loaded on the top. The folds had been made by cutting half through with a knife and various ways of strengthening these were tried with a marked effect. A good deal of observation then went on to find out where, on real structures, extra material was used or strengthening added to points liable to extra stress.

Almost always further investigations will arise from the starting experiment (use of other materials, different sizes, etc, asking 'what would happen if . . . ?'), and it will certainly be worth following these rather than trying to stick to this chapter as a text, which it is not intended to be.

Rigid, flexible and plastic things

No material is *really* rigid, but in practice one accepts an arbitrary standard of some kind. Sort out a collection of paper, card, flex, various plastics, wood, metals (wires and strips), rubber, Plasticine, cloth, glass, putty, etc, into:

Rigid   (samples which won't bend)

Flexible   (samples which bend and spring back)

Plastic   (samples which bend but don't spring back)

Plastics are not normally plastic, which is a bit confusing. Many are when they are heated (plastics is simply the name given to a whole group of synthetic materials). The Project's Unit on plastics would be of interest here.

Which of the above groups a material belongs to depends on its shape and size. Compare a thick electric cable with lighting flex, a copper tube with copper wire, a thin sheet of metal with thicker pieces and with a casting and a girder, a thick piece of plastic with a polythene bag, a tumbler or a piece of plate glass with a thin, drawn-out glass tube or glass fibre.

If the flexibility of a piece of wire is compared when it is straight and when formed into a spiral, this may lead to a lot of work on bouncing, springs and elasticity.

Does *plasticity*, ie the ability to deform without springing back, change with shape and size? Try it with Plasticine or clay.

Strong shapes and arrangements

What is usually needed is the strongest structure for the least amount of material. This is particularly so for structures for flying (see next chapter).

Arches and dome shapes
Flat card bridges may be compared with arches using any arbitrary weight standard such as coins or washers. High arches may be compared with flatter ones.

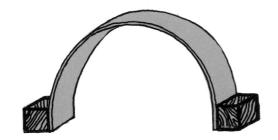

To test the strength of dome shapes one class tested egg shells.

What force is needed to break the shell?

Does the size of the egg make a difference?

Try various sizes of hen eggs and pullet eggs.

Are free-range eggs stronger than battery eggs?

Does the thickness of egg shells vary?

What ways are there of measuring a small thing like the thickness of a shell?

Can we invent some of our own?

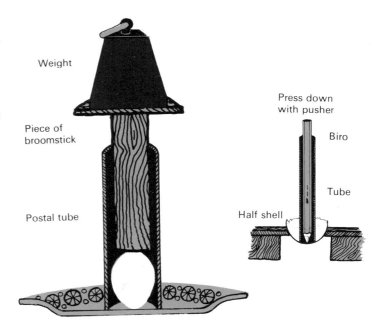

Weight

Piece of broomstick

Postal tube

Press down with pusher

Biro

Tube

Half shell

How much force must a chicken exert to get out?

The apparatus shown was used to try to find out.

But a chicken does not just press through.

What does it really do?

Planks and trusses

Children at Stage 2 may be interested in further experiments with plank bridges.

The interesting thing is to vary conditions:

a. Different lengths between the supports.

b. Different materials (eg balsa strip, hardboard, plywood).

c. Different scale of the experiment (eg use builder's plank, floorboard).

d. What difference does the thickness of the plank make?

In each case a scale may be erected behind the centre point and sag measured for different loadings. Plot a graph of sag against load.

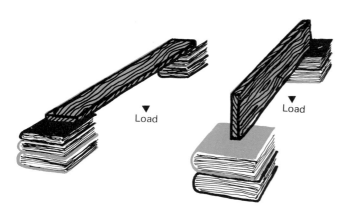

Will a plank support more flat or on edge? That is, what difference does the arrangement of the plank make?

Try this with a very thin piece of wood (ply or hardboard).

What difficulties are there in using a thin beam on its edge for a bridge?

Could you overcome them?

Some of the plank bridges tested may now be supported, by an arch of flexible material underneath, as shown, and the sag for various weights compared with earlier figures.

Instead of using weights for the force applied, it is often convenient to use a pusher-puller such as the one shown.

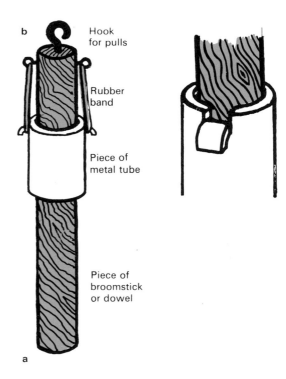

This can be made in many sizes and strengths for a multitude of purposes. Old TV aerials and the tubular framework of old garden chairs are convenient sources of metal tubing.

Holding the tube, end (*a*) can be used to push and a scale marked on the cylinder to measure it. End (*b*) can be used to measure pulls. Inverted, the gadget becomes a spring balance.

It prevents confusion to stick to arbitrary measures for a long time, ie simply to put marks along the cylinder at equal intervals and count them. If necessary, it can be calibrated in marbles, standard washers, nails or even bricks.

Round about Stage 2 level it might be sense to introduce some pusher-pullers which are marked in Newtons, simply saying that this is the 'real' unit used for measuring forces. Children will accept it arbitrarily just like others. To try to explain how it came about or relate it to kilograms-weight at this stage would be a great mistake. (See *Structures and forces, Stage 3*.) What we are trying to do is to compare the sizes of forces and we can arbitrarily use any unit we like at this stage in the same way that we can measure lengths in inches, millimetres or barleycorns.

Various lattice girders and trusses may be made from straws pinned or glued together, from balsa wood or from card strips fixed with paper fasteners. Weights may be placed on them to test to destruction.

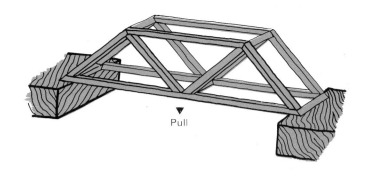

Pull

Where does the failure occur, in the material or at the joint?

Did the material break or buckle?

Could you design it better?

Are accurately made models stronger than 'rough' ones?

How does the load on the uprights change as the traffic crosses the bridge?

Try it out with the apparatus shown. Alternatively, a plank resting on two bathroom scales may be used, with children walking across as the traffic.

Cantilevers

Measure the sag of a cantilever with various loads, altering the variables as with the plank bridge (ie different lengths, thickness and material of the plank and different scale of experiment).

It is always exciting if the tests can be taken as far as the point of destruction.

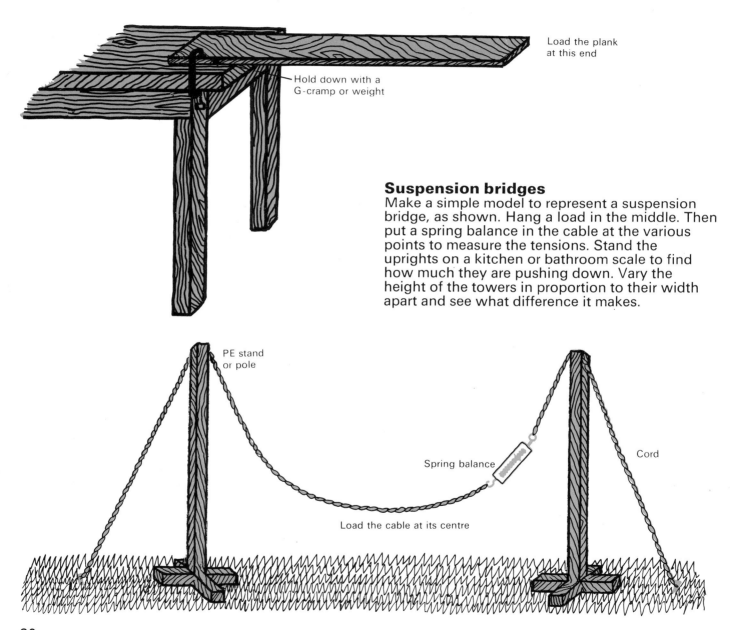

Load the plank at this end

Hold down with a G-cramp or weight

Suspension bridges

Make a simple model to represent a suspension bridge, as shown. Hang a load in the middle. Then put a spring balance in the cable at the various points to measure the tensions. Stand the uprights on a kitchen or bathroom scale to find how much they are pushing down. Vary the height of the towers in proportion to their width apart and see what difference it makes.

PE stand or pole

Spring balance

Cord

Load the cable at its centre

Folds, bends and girders

The relation of strength to size, shape and structure offers a great deal of interesting investigation.

Various shapes may be supported at their ends and tested by loading in the middle.

How does a card turned up at the edges compare with a flat piece?

Do the proportions matter?

If you extend the idea to make a tube how strong is that?

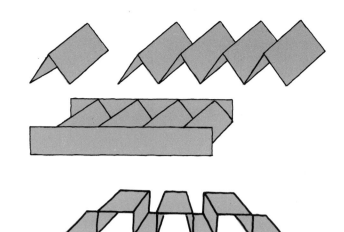

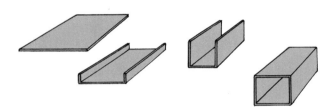

Children could find out where there is a real bridge made like this and all about the man who made it and how it was done. (In the Menai bridge the trains go through the tube but many other bridges use box sections not so obviously, eg the Queen's bridge at Perth, in which the road is carried above three box girders.)

What else can you find out about the effect of folding on strength?

Compare a plain sheet of paper with a pleated sheet.

How are you going to test them fairly?

Does the size of the pleat make any difference?

What difference does it make if you glue a strip of paper across the ends?

Can you find out how much stronger corrugated card is than three flat pieces of the same material? How much more material does it need? (There are several ways of answering the last question; weighing is perhaps the easiest.)

Sometimes corrugated card is made as a double sandwich. Has this any advantage?

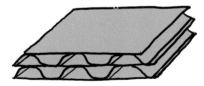

Does corrugated card bend equally well in all directions?

Could you invent a material which is 'strong both ways'?

Corrugated roofing material (metal and plastic) could be investigated for bending strength and compared with flat sheets.

Try bending a Meccano strip and an angle girder which are both made of the same thickness of the same material.

What different shapes of girders can be found?

Make cardboard models of girders and test their strength.

What difference does shape make?

What difference does proportion make?

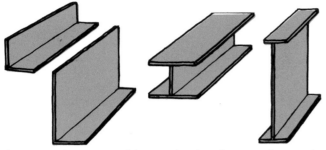

One teacher was able to obtain pieces of actual girders to look at and said that this made the work much more exciting and interesting.

Strength of tubes
Do tubes make good girders? Make a sheet of paper into a tube and test its strength.

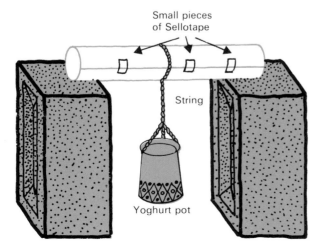

Small pieces of Sellotape

String

Yoghurt pot

Sand may be poured into the pot until the tube buckles.

What can you find out about the strength of tubes of different diameter?

What things must you watch to make it a fair test?

Use the same kind of paper and the same sized sheet each time to form tubes of different diameters. The large diameter tubes will have thin walls, the small diameter thick walls.

What size gives maximum rigidity?

Plot a graph of load to buckle against external diameter. The result may be a little surprising.

One school was interested in what happened if the tubes were not loaded symmetrically. This comes up again in the following experiment.

Try the tubes vertically. Again try different diameters. Does the *length* of the tube matter? When the tube gets really wide you will need a bucket for the sand. What happens if you load one of the wider tubes off-centre? This can most

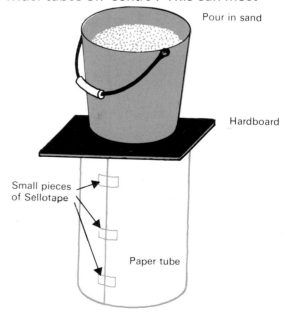

Pour in sand

Hardboard

Small pieces of Sellotape

Paper tube

easily be done by putting a partition in the bucket and pouring sand into one side only.

Has the result any significance for real structures?

Are symmetrical structures stronger?

Where are tubes used in bridges and buildings you have seen?

Where else are they used for strength?

Bundles

Use dried plant stems, straws or paper tubes. What weight (or push) is needed at the centre of one to make it bend 5 mm. Always use the same length between supports. Are all stems (etc) the same? Get an average.

Next try two stems held with a rubber band at both ends. Then continue with three, four and so on. Are two stems twice as strong as one, three, three times as strong, etc?

Leonardo da Vinci experimented with bundles of rushes. He found that when he bound a lot together each single rush supported twelve times more weight than it could alone. Do you get a result like this?

Instead of having rubber bands just at the ends, try binding the stems firmly so that they touch for their whole length. What difference does it make?

After this it will be obvious to try gluing the stems and straws together. What results do you get now?

How are strong bundles used:

a. On the roofs of old cottages?
b. In modern bridges?
c. In boats?

Laminations

Compare the strength of a single piece of card or balsa sheet with a double thickness pasted or glued, then a treble thickness and so on.

For Stage 2 do it more accurately, eg have a standard length of card between supports, measure sag for a standard weight; and plot a graph of sag against number of laminations. Is it a straight line?

Compare the strength of a strip of plywood with a piece of ordinary wood of the same thickness. (It is rather exciting to do a destruction test in this case, using bricks for weights.)

Look at the grain of the wood that makes up the laminations.

Fixing things together

Things sometimes need fixing together so that they can move: for instance, the ways the arms and legs of a puppet are fixed to its body, or a toy windmill is fixed to its stick. The easiest way to do it is to use a pin, a nail, a rivet, a paper fastener or a loose nut and bolt—just *one*, so that the parts can turn.

Of course, most moving joints like those in our knees or shoulders, or in the steering of a car, are much more complicated.

Often things need fixing rigidly. If you fix together frameworks with loose joints (eg card strips with paper fasteners) you find an interesting thing about the three-sided one—it is the only one which is rigid.

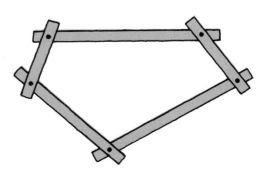

In how many ways could you make a five-sided framework rigid?

Can it be done using string? (It depends in what direction the push is.)

Look at structures in which triangles have been made for rigidity.

What about a tetrahedron, which, in a way, is a three-dimensional triangle. Is this strong and rigid?

Make some to see.

Can you find structures in which this shape is used?

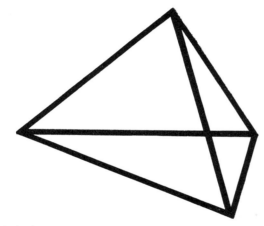

A tetrahedron

A simple way to make a firm fixing is to use *two* nails, bolts, rivets, etc, or to fix one bolt really tight with a spring washer to stop it shaking loose again.

Children can find out how firm joints are made in scaffolding; look for the kinds of joints used to make furniture rigid, and for bolted, riveted and welded joints in bridges, ships, cars, railway lines, etc.

Can you find out if a lap joint is as strong as a butt joint?

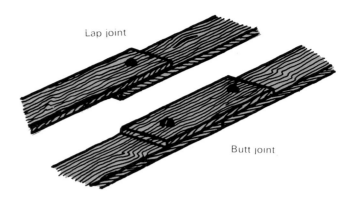

Lap joint

Butt joint

Compare the strength of a nailed, screwed or bolted joint with that of the material *without* a joint (usually it is only about fifteen per cent).

Glues
Nowadays we have a great variety of glues which are very convenient for joining.

To start with, make a collection and test whether a glue will do what the packet says it will do. Some claim that they can 'stick anything to anything'.

Are some glues better than others for certain materials?

Is there a glue which will fix metal to glass?

Children can devise tests for comparing different kinds. All the variables other than 'kind of glue' must be eliminated; the same materials must be stuck together, we must have the same smoothness of the two faces, the same area glued, the same test done. One test is shown.

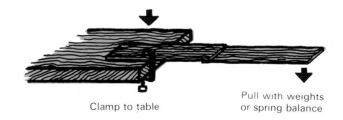

Clamp to table

Pull with weights or spring balance

Do you get the same results for tests done as shown here (In this case there will be no leverage along the front edge of the join) :

Fix firmly

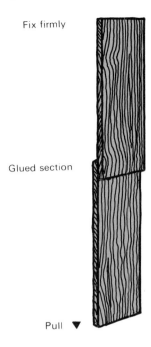

Glued section

Pull ▼

One of the best tests has been found to be using the first method, but instead of overlapping the joint to glue only the butt-ends.

Allow the glue to dry thoroughly before testing. (See also *Working with wood, Stages 1 & 2.*)

Demonstrating the strength of a modern glue

The pull of the earth

From the day we drop our first toy over the edge of the pram, or certainly from the time of our first attempt to stand we are well aware that the earth pulls things.

Now that space capsules are commonplace, most children know that our weight is simply the force with which the earth pulls us and that we do not have the same weight in space or on the moon although there is the same amount of us—the same *mass*.

All things fall at the same rate

This can only be shown satisfactorily on a large scale. Objects of contrasting weight like a brick and a small stone can be dropped at the same time from a flat roof or high window on to a metal sheet below. Obviously proper precautions must be taken. Perhaps the best way to start them together is to tip them both off a piece of wood. Many objects should be tried. The effect of air resistance on light objects will be noticed.

The fall of a sheet of paper should be compared with that of a similar piece screwed up into a tight ball.

This will, no doubt, lead to work on parachutes and perhaps discussion on why a mouse can fall from the top of a haystack without harm, the attempts of 'birdmen' to fly, and modern gliders (see the Unit *Science from toys, Stages 1 & 2*).

Walls and foundations

Piles of toy building bricks easily fall over. A young child soon finds that they must be stacked vertically so that the weight-force pushes straight down through all the bricks below. It helps to prevent toppling if the base is wider than the top. The heavier the bricks, the firmer is the pile but you must have a good foundation to take the weight.

The action of foundations can easily be shown by

pushing downwards on a model wall standing on soil or sand.

The effect with the first model is compared with the second, which has a foundation strip. The difference can easily be felt.

The same push may be applied to each model using weights or a pusher and the depth to which the wall sinks in the sand may be compared. In

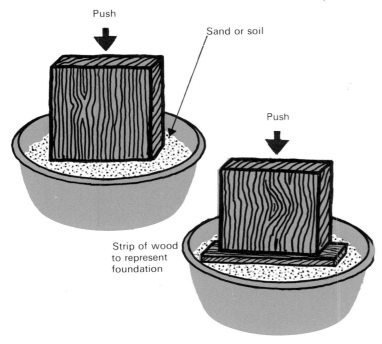

Push

Sand or soil

Push

Strip of wood to represent foundation

The following experiment gives useful experience of pressure. Push a pencil into Plasticine or card (*a*) point first, (*b*) flat end first.

At first the experience and observation are enough. Later some encouragement can be given to devise a means of applying a constant force on the pencil and measuring the depth of the hole.

The apparatus shown on the drawing below may also be used to gain experiences about the idea of pressure.

Various cross-sections of dowel rod have a flat piece of wood screwed to the top. The frame holds them steady while they are weighted at the top to see how far each is driven into a block of Plasticine.

Using the same force (eg the weight of a brick) each time it is easy to see how pressure is related to area. Later perhaps the area of the end of the dowel and the depth of the hole may be measured and a graph plotted of weight against depth of hole made in the clay, drawing a separate line on the graph for each different cross-sectional area. (Some teachers may prefer to use square section rods so that the area may be more easily calculated.)

the first case the *pressure* is greater because the push acts over a small area. In the second case the push is spread over a large area and the pressure is less.

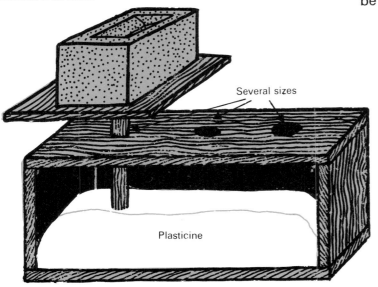

Several sizes

Plasticine

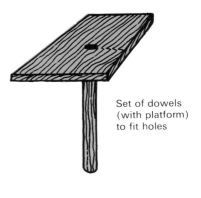

Set of dowels (with platform) to fit holes

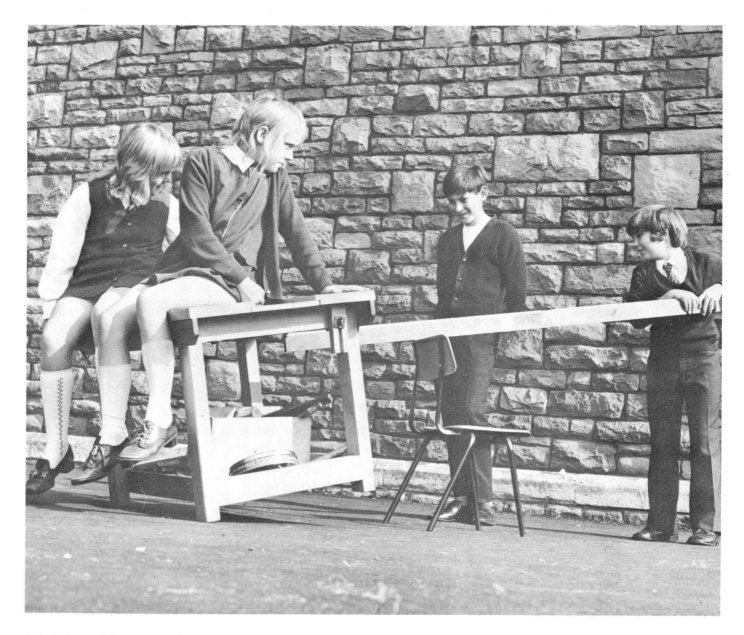

Making things easier to lift

When making structures there are many things too heavy to lift ourselves. What simple machines are used to help? Children can experiment themselves.

Levers

It is very easy to lift a table or a child on a chair using a lever of timber or to lift a heavy box with an iron bar. Look for uses of levers in everyday life.

Experience of the law of the lever could be had in ways such as:

1. Pushing to close a door at different distances from the hinges with a pusher and recording.

What do you notice each time about push multiplied by distance from the hinge?

2. Finding how the pull changes as the position of the pencil is changed with this arrangement.

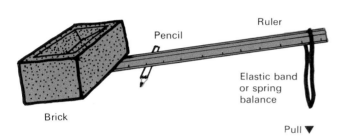

Brick · Pencil · Ruler · Elastic band or spring balance · Pull ▼

3. Using a balance beam (often in mathematical apparatus) and balancing a weight on one side, with twice the weight and so on, on the other side.

It is a very useful occupation at this stage to devise balances of as many different designs as

A balance for small weights

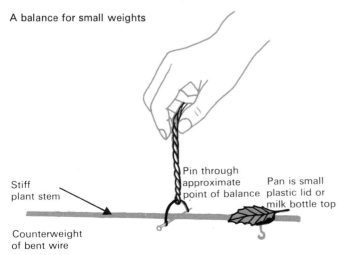

Stiff plant stem · Counterweight of bent wire · Pin through approximate point of balance · Pan is small plastic lid or milk bottle top

possible. It is something of a challenge to demand that one at least should be big enough to weigh teacher and one delicate enough to weigh a leaf or a seed.

A simple balance made from a straw is described in the Nuffield O-level Physics scheme (*Guide to experiments I*).

A rubber-band balance is very easily made:

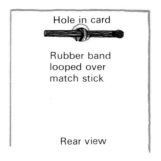

Hole in card · Rubber band looped over match stick · Rear view

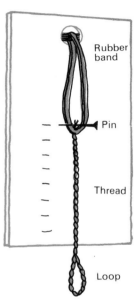

Rubber band · Pin · Thread · Loop

Small cartons or lids may be hung on if a pan is needed. Calibrations are made for each balance as required, in units invented by children (dried peas, marbles, nails, etc) or later in grams.

Slopes
A trolley with a heavy load is hard to lift on to a table but can easily be pulled up a sloping plank.

Lift a toy lorry vertically with a piece of elastic and note how much the elastic stretches. Next pull it up a slope by means of the elastic and note the stretch again (or use a spring balance). Try different slopes and different weights in the lorry. If you want to lift a heavy weight with a small pull what kind of slope must you have? But a long

69

slope takes a lot of room, so the slope is often wound in a spiral round a column. Perhaps children could work a screw-jack from a car, and experience putting in wood screws.

Pulleys
A pulley is very convenient for changing the direction of a pull. Two pulleys (eg clothes airer type or Meccano) can be arranged to show mechanical advantage. This is often used in cranes. Notice how much further you have to pull the string to lift the weight the same distance.

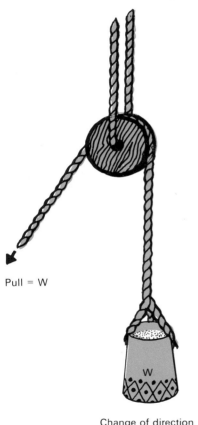

Pull = W

Change of direction

Mechanical advantage

Pull = ½W

The force of the wind

Much interesting experimental work can be done by children with a wind speed measurer. Wind speeds can be noted from day to day (perhaps as part of a weather interest) and wind speeds round about buildings, near trees, hedges, etc, recorded and compared.

One simple instrument may be constructed as shown. There is a better, though more delicate, one in the *Solarbo Book of Balsa Models* (see Bibliography).

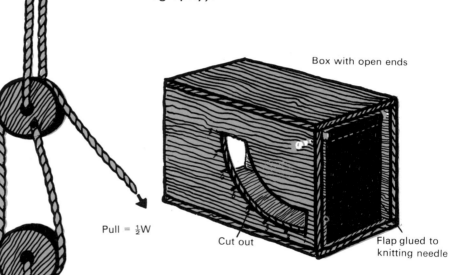

Box with open ends

Cut out

Flap glued to knitting needle

For a long time no one took much notice about the force of the wind on structures, but it can be very great and has caused many disasters (eg to the Tay Bridge and Tacoma Narrows Bridge).

Even when the effect is not so terrible, wind forces cause many problems. Tall buildings sway quite a lot; the GPO tower, for example, sways over 200 mm in a strong gale. From an engineering point of view the sway doesn't matter much but how much can people stand?

Another problem with tall buildings is the strange air currents they cause round about them. An example is shown.

It may be possible to take wind vanes and wind-speed measurers into spaces between tall buildings.

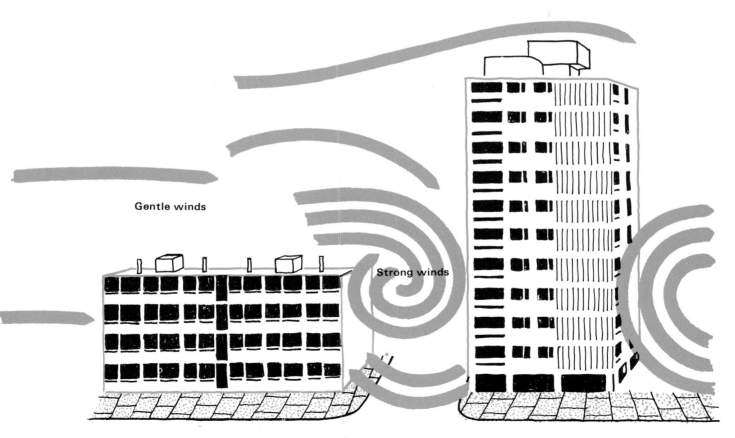

Gentle winds

Strong winds

Streamlining

Can you blow out a candle flame standing behind a card as shown?

Which way does the air current flow on the candle side of the card when you blow?

What happens when you replace the flat card by a cylinder?

Of course, to be fair, the vertical section of the cylinder must have the same area as the flat card. Perhaps the easiest method is to use a can for the cylinder and to cut the flat card equal to the can in height and in width equal to the can's diameter.

Some children may be able to tackle the following.

Suspend a table tennis ball from a thread by means of glue. Blow on it with a fan or vacuum cleaner and estimate the angle the thread makes with the vertical.

Next find the diameter of the ball and its cross-sectional area and cut a rectangular piece of balsa wood with the same area.

Then adjust the weight of the balsa wood by cutting from the back or adding a bit of Plasticine until it weighs the same as the table tennis ball. (Later it would be interesting to see if weight makes any difference, but at the moment we are concerned with being fair.) Suspend the balsa wood by the same length of thread, blow with the same 'blower' and see what angle the thread makes with the vertical now.

Try other shapes. For example, add a conical tail to the ball and the block to see if that makes any difference.

What appears to be the most streamlined shape you can make?

No doubt, the topic of streamlining will also lead to work on cars, speed, etc, and discussion on the use of wind-tunnels.

For the sake of good English the absurdity of the use of the word 'streamlined' to describe such things as lamps, cookers and prams should be pointed out.

After hearing or reading of the improved design for the decking of the Severn Bridge after aerodynamic experiments, children might like to make a model along with one of the older type of design, hang them from a beam and compare their stability when blown with a fan or vacuum cleaner, or simply by the mouth.

These models are probably best constructed from balsa wood. As is shown in the drawing, the Severn Bridge also had a different arrangement of suspending wires which was also designed to reduce flutter. Experiments may be made to see if this is the effect with the model.

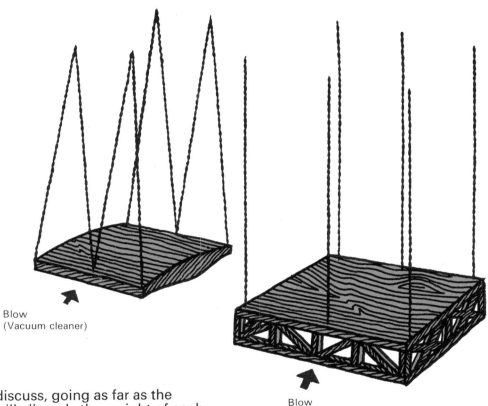

Blow
(Vacuum cleaner)

Blow

There is much to discuss, going as far as the children's ability will allow. Is the weight of each model the same? Have we not got *four* suspension wires on the one to three on the other? Suppose we have four on each. (On the real bridges less suspending cable is used on the Severn Bridge than on the Forth Bridge.)

The decking section of the Severn Bridge may suggest an inverted aeroplane wing and lead to the way wind forces produce lift in aeroplanes (see next chapter).

9 Natural structures

It would be a mistake to consider only man-made structures. Living things have evolved structures which are so complicated, and often so efficient and beautiful, that the best of man's efforts look clumsy and crude in comparison. The system of skeleton, limbs, joints and muscles in any mammal is a superb structure for its purpose; the structure of a tree, a dragonfly's wings or a water flea's antennae are something to wonder at. But then 'nature' has been at it for a good many millions of years; insects were probably flying 400 million years ago, which makes them a thousand times as old as the human species.

Just as man has learned from the towers which fell down and bridges which collapsed in a high wind, so the process of evolution wipes out the failures and develops the successful lines.

The structure of animals

Animals without hard parts
There are jellyfishes and sea anemones to look at for some. Inland, fresh-water hydra are common if rather small. It is worth washing out some samples of pond weed in water in a glass tank and looking for hydra clinging to the glass on the side towards the light.

Slugs at least are available to everyone.

Can you find different kinds?

Let them crawl on glass or Perspex to find out how they move.

How *fast* do they move?

What is the slime for?

How do they breathe?

How do they see?

Exactly how do they draw in their eyes when you touch them?

What do the other two feelers do?

What do slugs eat?

Do they prefer lettuce to cabbage?

How do they eat?

When do they eat?

How much do they eat?

Do they have homes to return to?

Eggs (small pearly spheres) can often be found in soil and compost heaps and will hatch if kept in a tube of moist soil indoors. Worms are also worth investigating. No less a scientist than Charles Darwin thought so.*

Look at the segments and count them.

Do all worms have the same number?

* *Charles Darwin*, The Formation of Vegetable Mould Through the Action of Worms With Observations on Their Habits, *Faber*.

How exactly does a worm move along?

What is its shortest length?

What is its longest length?

The worm's bristles make quite a scraping noise on a sheet of brown paper and one can try to see them by holding the paper up against the light.

How do you tell the front from the rear end?

No eyes can be found but a worm enclosed in a dark box reacts to light from a bright torch.

Does each end react equally?

Worms may be kept easily in a deep container of damp soil. By putting leaves, carrot, onion, etc,

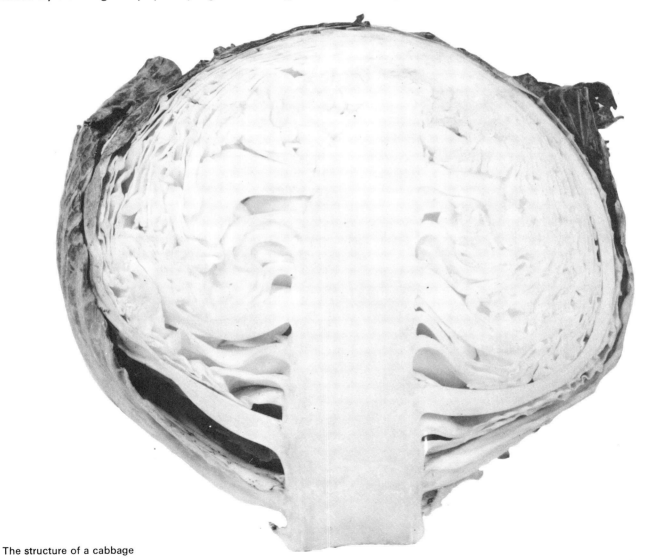

The structure of a cabbage

on the surface, food preferences can be discovered, and if the soil is arranged in layers to start with, the way in which worms churn up the soil is seen.

Perhaps the easiest arrangement is a large jar surrounded by a cylinder of dark paper which can slide up to allow inspection of the contents. A large jar will take two or three fairly big worms. It is important to see that the soil is moist but not water-logged.

Teachers will find a great deal to help them with work on invertebrates in the Unit *Minibeasts*.

Animals with hard parts outside
Children are able to look at a large variety of these, eg tortoises, beetles and other insects. Look for joints in the body which make movement possible and, with a lens, the structure of jointed legs.

A ladybird is a good beetle for watching how the flying wings pack under the hard wing cases. Just how they fold in is a great wonder.

What happens when an animal with a hard outside grows bigger? Stick insects are useful for showing moulting easily.

Animals with skeletons
There are so many of these: pets, zoo animals, ourselves. It is easy to obtain skeletons of fishes and most of the bones of chickens and perhaps rabbits from the kitchen, or by boiling off the flesh. It is rather too lengthy and detailed a job for junior children to put a skeleton together but parts such as a wing, a leg, a rib cage, might be tried by simple glueing.

Cut a shin bone across with a saw (perhaps the butcher will do it for you).

What is the thickness of actual bone?

Do different animals have bones different in structure and weight?

Is a chicken's leg bone made the same way as its wing bone?

Does an animal twice as big have bones twice as big in diameter, length, thickness of bone and weight?

Just what do we mean by twice as big?

Large bones from the butchers are useful in finding how joints in the skeleton work.

Skeleton of a frog

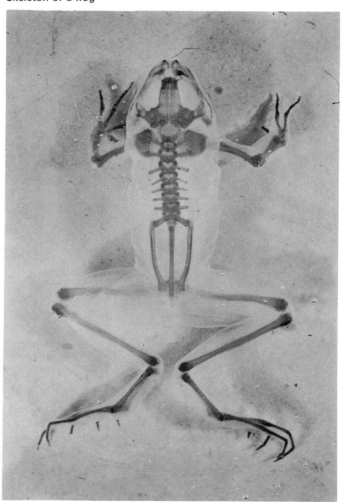

What forces does a bone have to withstand?

Do these affect the shape and structure of a bone?

Children will be able to look at the large keeled breast-bone from a chicken. It is strengthened like a girder, with the keel bone at right angles to the main structure. This makes it strong enough to take the pull of the wing muscles (the flesh we eat), yet it is still very light.

It is interesting to compare the strength of bone with metal or wood of about the same cross-section, by loading to breaking point, and to compare bones of different animals. Obviously here we are restricted to smaller bones in the classroom.

The skeleton alone is not able to give an animal stiffness and resist forces. It has to be held in position and controlled by muscles which pull on it, always balancing one another and automatically

Skeleton of a horse

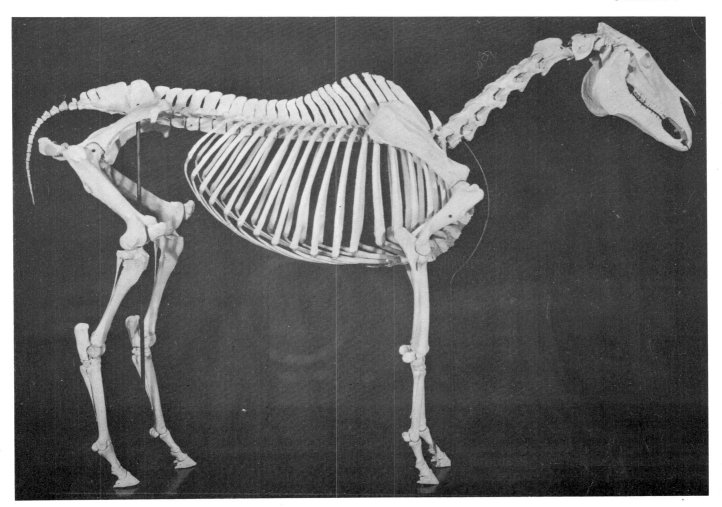

adjusting the pull according to the load.

Some teachers might like to discuss the structure of the skin, which, while being hardwearing, antiseptic and almost waterproof, is beautifully stretchable and self-healing. Children can look at their own skin with a lens and watch what happens when they get cuts and bruises.

What different outer surfaces do other animals have?

Structures for flying

Compare the weight and structure of a bird's wing bone with other bones. Flying needs especially light strong structures.

Look at insects' wings, birds' wings (bats' wings if possible) and aeroplane wings. How is the problem solved?

Have a competition to make the best glider from, say, expanded polystyrene ceiling tiles or post-cards.

How are they to be tested?

What do we mean by best?

Is it the one which flies furthest, the one which stays up the longest time, or the best at aerobatics?

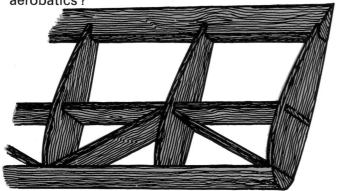

The structure of a model aeroplane wing

Make flying model aeroplanes.

How do you get a strong light framework with a strong light skin?

There is no doubt that the interest here will, for many children, be in air and flight, and work should obviously go along that line. They might look at the shape of a bird's wings and the shape of aeroplane wings and how these shapes give lift. Another interest might be the history of flight. Hot-air balloons could be made and many schools have had great success with them, usually after a few failures to begin with.

Here is a design used by a London school. Don't forget to choose a day with little if any wind and that take-off *must* be supervised.

Eight panels of tissue paper are needed:

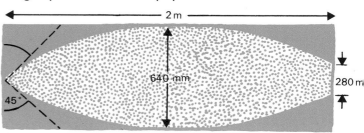

(It is best to cut out a template in newspaper or brown paper and work from this.)

A square frame is made of $\frac{1}{4}$-in [5–6-mm] balsa wood strips with diagonals of stiff thin wire (thin piano wire).

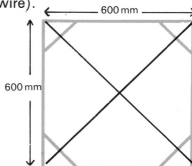

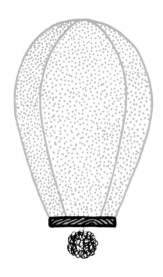

What are feathers like?

How does the structure of a feather used for flying differ from one used for body covering?

Compare the thickness and strength of the middle rib and of the barbs.

With a low-power microscope or a good lens one can investigate how the barbs of wing feathers lock together.

Kinds of feathers

Cotton wool, soaked in meths, is hooked on to the crosswires and lighted.

Hold the frame until a lift is felt.

Work in open spaces where there is no danger of igniting anything else! Indoors, try filling the balloon with hot air from a hair-drier or fan-type electric heater.

A study of air would need a Unit for itself, but it has been fairly well covered in many books. The point here is, that while our objective may have to do with structures the right thing might be to modify our ideas according to our children's needs.

How heavy is an insect, a bird, a flying model plane?

How do they compare with other things about the same size which do not fly? (eg a slug, a mouse, a model car).

Weigh as many as you can.

Competition model planes often weigh about 1 gramme and yet have a wing span of only a little short of a metre!

Structures animals build

Some of these are easy for children at almost any school to look at:

Bee cells in a honeycomb.

Spiders' webs.

Nest of the dormouse

What different kinds are there?

What different places do the different spiders choose?

Where does the spider hide?

What does it do when it catches something?

Spiders' egg cocoons (look in cracks of wood in spring, especially any pieces lying in grass).

Mole hills.

Birds' nests. When the birds have finished with these, find out exactly what they used for building and in what proportions.

How many times their own weight had the birds carried?

How do different nests differ?

How does the bird know what to do?

Please do not perpetuate the idea that a bird's nest is its *home*!

Nests which pet mice, hamsters, etc, build.

Caddis cases.

There are others which may only be available occasionally: ant hills, a wasp's nest, a badger set, perhaps the nests of mason bees or the nest of a dormouse.

Pictures of other animal-built structures should be used, eg beaver dams, termites' nests, trapdoor spiders, coral.

The structure of plants

Why is a tree so stiff and strong? (See the Unit *Trees*.)

Collect stems of plants and test their stiffness.

Hold them horizontally by fixing one end, and add small weights (eg bits of Plasticine) to the other. Equal lengths are used and the amount of dip measured. Cut the stems across to see how they are constructed.

Which are woody and which not?

Which are hollow?

What is the shape of the cross-section?

Can you find a square one, a triangular one or one which is ribbed round the outside?

Look at the pith of elder stems and in rushes. Try to make whistles from the hollow stems of hog-weed.

Stems without much woody tissue will wilt. If a freshly cut stem is fixed horizontally, being held at one end, the wilting can be measured. On a

Natural formations: Trevaunance Cove, Cornwall

paper fixed behind the stem, the position of the free end can be marked at intervals of, say, five minutes. Compare many stems, cutting them across to see the differences of structure.

What are the variables?

What do you have to make the same to keep the test as fair as possible?

Does standing the end in water stiffen the stems again?

(Rhubarb is handy to work with.)

Stiffness in these cases is due to pressure inside the cell walls. This is called *turgidity*, and a nice demonstration is to have a bicycle inner tube and to compare it flat and at various stages of being blown up.

There are many interesting applications of this idea. Igloo tents are set up by inflating their ribs. Inflatable rubber dinghies are well known and some very interesting buildings have been tried which are virtually a thin plastic skin kept stiff by a pump which maintains a slightly greater air pressure inside than outside.

When an adult butterfly, dragonfly or mayfly breaks from its pupa, its crumpled wings are stretched by a similar inflation of the veins, but in this case the process is non-reversible and the wings harden.

Water goes up a plant stem. Does it go up the whole stem? Put many stems (with leaves still on, of course) in water with a little red ink and later cut across to see where the water goes. What different patterns do you get? A nice easy stem to use is a stick of celery but try as many as you can. See what happens to a white carnation flower or a large daisy.

Other natural structures

In quarries and road, rail or river cuttings we can look at the structure of the first few feet of the earth's crust.

Why is it in layers (strata)?

Why are they bent?

How were rocks formed in the first place?

How many kinds of rock can be found locally and what is the internal structure of them?

Break some open with a hammer and look with a lens to see if you can see anything about how they were formed. Can you see any crystals or fossil shapes, for example?

This will certainly lead to discussions on geological time (see the Unit *Time*), evolution, fossils, crystals and (particularly in limestone districts) to solubility.

An interest of this kind could very easily arise from looking at kinds of stone used locally for buildings.

The structure of soil is well worth looking at; how it changes with depth and locality and its different qualities as a plant-growing medium. Much simple experimental work on soil has been described in books and will not be repeated here.

10 Structure and pattern

Structures, both natural and man-made, frequently show patterns.

There is no doubt that some of the most aesthetically pleasing patterns are those that arise from the fundamental structure behind them, the fan vaulting in King's College Chapel, for example, or the golden branches of a weeping willow.

Perhaps all that can be done here is to suggest a few structural patterns to look for and hope that it will start our interest. There is a lot of science to follow up in all the things mentioned if anyone wishes to do so.

I suppose science could, in one sense, be defined as *looking for patterns*. Some of the most remarkable ones discovered in recent years have been the molecular patterns of the proteins and DNA.

Some natural patterns to investigate

Leaves
How many shapes of leaves can be found?

In what pattern are they arranged on the stem?

In what way does the plant hold them to get most light? (A pattern is especially noticeable in trees and shrubs.)

Does the sunlight shining through leaves make a pattern on the ground?

How many different patterns can be found for the *edges* of leaves?

What are the two main groups of vein patterns in leaves?

Make scribble prints of leaf-vein patterns.

Flowers
The variety of flower patterns is huge. Start with some simple regular ones, perhaps petals only at first, eg Black-Eyed Susan, a periwinkle, a dog rose.

The pattern of marks on petals is always interesting, particularly in violas, lilies and gladioli.

Fungi
In autumn the pattern of gills or spore tubes can be looked at and spore prints made as shown.

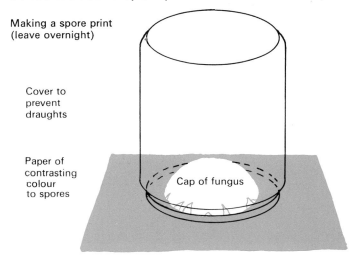

Making a spore print
(leave overnight)

Cover to prevent draughts

Paper of contrasting colour to spores

Cap of fungus

Shells

The interesting structure of shells arises from the fact that they are built up by adding to the open end as the animal grows bigger, resulting usually in wonderful expanding spiral whorls. Often shells have quite intricate growths and varied coloured patterns. (Spirals might be a topic to take up. Look for spirals in climbing plants, staircases, etc.) There are several fresh-water snails for keeping in school.

Is the shell like a spire or a Catherine-wheel?

What shape is the opening?

For the spire shells, when you look at the opening, does the shell wind to the left or the right?

Snails that live in grass

A pond snail

Does the snail close the opening with a door or not?

Watch the snails eating the green algae on the walls of a tank. Watch them move. Do they ever walk along the under surface of the water?

Why do they not sink?

Do they sink when you first put them into water?

How do they breathe under water?

No doubt they will lay eggs on the sides of the vessel you keep them in. The development may be watched with a hand lens. The interesting thing is that the young snails hatch complete with a tiny shell which remains as the very tip of the shell for the adult.

Land snails can be watched outside or kept in dishes of damp rich soil with cabbage leaves, lettuce leaves, grass, etc. Keep a lid on the dish!

Sea shells and shells from other countries make a marvellous collection of structural patterns. The patterns of tortoise shells are interesting too.

Caddis cases

Caddis larvae build cases in many ways depending on their species. Can you find cases made of sand grains, bits of stem, tiny plant bits woven like a basket, folded leaves?

A caddis fly larva

Crystals

Snowflakes can be caught on a black cloth in winter and looked at quickly before they melt.

Crystals of sugar, alum, perhaps copper sulphate, can be grown by letting a strong solution evaporate slowly. Crystals can be looked for in rock samples.

Fingerprints

We all have patterns of lines on the skin of our finger tips. It would be interesting to find out if it is true that everyone in a class has a different pattern.

Wing patterns

A museum collection would help considerably to study different patterns of wings; those of butterflies, moths and other insects and those of birds.

Some man-made patterns

Walls

The arrangement of stone, bricks, flints and wood. The texture of surfaces and pattern of shadows.

Roofs

The pattern of tiles and slates, thatch, etc. The shapes of the roofs of factories.

Windows and doorways

The pattern they make in blocks and terraces. The care taken over proportion in some architectural periods.

The arrangement of struts in girders of bridges, buildings, cranes, pylons, etc.

The lines and patterns of fields, crops and cultivations. The weaves and colours of cloth.

One could investigate and use structures which *make* patterns such as the Spirograph and sand pendulum (see the Unit *Time*) and try to invent others.

Pictures are also a great help. We can look at the patterns of diatoms, corals and tropical shells, insects and plants. One can compare a picture of the blades of a turbine with one of a fossil trilobite.

Symmetry

There are three kinds of symmetry which children at this stage will be able to recognise.

i. Rotational.

ii. Translational (ie repeating pattern).

iii. Bilateral.

Look for symmetry in three-dimensional structures too.

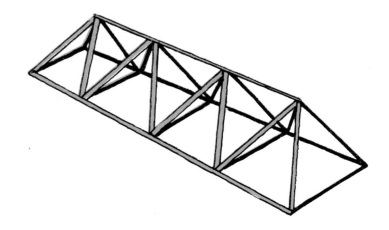

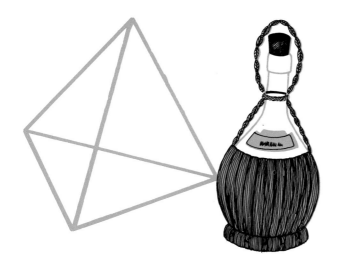

and change it into a rotationally symmetrical pattern; for example:

Then into a translational symmetrical pattern:

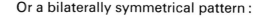

Natural objects are usually only approximately symmetrical (for example, the two sides of one's face).

Some things for children to do about symmetry

Look for symmetry; decide what kind it is.

Are there any things which show more than one type?

Are there any which *seem* symmetrical but must belong to a different group which we have not thought of?

Make symmetrical designs.

Make a non-symmetrical pattern. For example:

Or a bilaterally symmetrical pattern:

Make blot patterns by folding paper with wet ink or paint on it.

Fold paper in various ways and cut pieces out. Open out to find the kind of symmetry produced.

Make paper chains.

Find symmetrical patterns in the shape of printed poetry and the sound of spoken poetry.

Find rhythms in music (clapping) and look at written music to find symmetry in sets of notes, etc.

Look for patterns in animal behaviour.

11 Bibliography

Gordon, J. E., *The New Science of Strong Materials or Why you don't fall through the floor*, Pelican. (A most helpful and amusing book on strength of materials including modern ones and glues.)

Shirley-Smith, H., *The World's Great Bridges*, Phoenix.

Overman, M., *Roads, Bridges and Tunnels*, Aldus.

Giles, J., *Bridges and Men*, Cassell.
(These three have most useful background material on types of bridges and their history.)

Morgan, W., *The Elements of Structure*, Pitman.
(Good background knowledge for teachers.)

Pannell, J. P. M., *An Illustrated History of Civil Engineering*, Thames and Hudson.

Potter, M. A., *Homes*, Murray.

Pevsner, N., *The Sources of Modern Architecture and Design*, Thames and Hudson.

Doherty, C. H., *Science on the Building Site*, and *Science Builds the Bridges*, Brockhampton Press.

Goldwater, D., *Bridges and How they are Built*, Worlds Work.

Henry, D., and Jerome, J. A., *Modern British Bridges*, CR Books.

The Appearance of Bridges, Ministry of Transport HMSO. (Relates engineering and aesthetics.)

Project (An engineering magazine published three times a year by the Central Office of Information for DES)

Solarbo Book of Balsa Models, Model and Allied Publications Ltd.

Davey, N., *A History of Building Materials*, Phoenix.

Mobiles, American Elementary Science Study Series, Heinemann.

Geary, K., *Make and Find Out* (four books), Macmillan. (Structures for flying, etc, which can be made by children.)

12 Materials and aids

Film loop
Tacoma Narrows Bridge Collapse. Ealing Film Loop No. 80–218.

'Art straws'
These are 18 in [457 mm] long in two diameters and sold in cases of about 2000. Available from: Sweetheart (Bristol) Ltd, College Road, Fishponds, Bristol BS16 2HR.

Bamboo poles
Example of sizes: 6 ft × 1 in, 9 ft × 1½ in, 8 ft × 1 in, 12 ft × 1½ in. [approx. 1·8 m × 25 mm, 2·7 m × 38 mm, 2·4 m × 25 mm, 3·6 m × 28 mm.] Available from: Jacobs, Young and Westbury Ltd, JYW House, Bridge Road, Haywards Heath, Sussex.

Large carpet stores may sometimes have them (they are used for winding rolls of carpets on).

Other materials
The following is a list of materials mentioned in the unit which are probably outside the normal range of supplies in a school:

Pipe cleaners
Expanded polystyrene tiles
A thick block of expanded polystyrene 100–150 mm [4–6 in] (builder's merchants)
Garden wire and florist's wire
Piano wire of several different gauges (model shops)
Garden canes
Strong sisal cord
Polycell paste
Distemper brush
Several buckets, bowls and plastic dishes (collect margarine packs)

A supply of balsa wood: strips, thin sheets and blocks
Balsa cement
Several craft knives
A few builder's planks
Cement
Sand
Gravel
G-cramps 2–4 in [50–100 mm] opening are most useful.
Washers of all sizes, especially large ones about 25 mm [1 in] diameter.
A supply of timber: strips, plyboard, blockboard, hardboard
Dowel-rod of different diameters 1 in–¼ in [30 mm–5 mm]
Several thermometers, 0–110° C
Polythene bags
A collection of metal samples
A collection of plastics samples
A collection of wood samples
As big a collection of different glues as possible
Weights: probably more will be called for than is usually available, especially in primary schools. They are expensive to buy. Often arbitrary weights, eg, bricks, coins, nails, washers, are suitable. Containers such as coffee cans, tablet tubes, even plastic bags can be made up into standard weights with sand.
Spring balances: bathroom scales, household scales and laboratory spring balances. The latter are expensive and often not very effective. If you can afford the tubular type get those. You need a range—but probably only one set.
Make a lot of 'pusher-pullers'.
Brass paper fasteners
Large sheets of tissue paper
A supply of Meccano parts is always useful.

Tools

Usual woodworking tools: Hammers, saws, drill (with bits), Surform tool, Stanley knife, small Eclipse hacksaws and a large one (with spare blades), screwdrivers, chisels, mallet, files, pliers. A selection of nails, screws, bolts and nuts. Also: cup-hooks, plumbline, spirit level, builder's trowel, try-square.

Objectives for children learning science
Guide lines to keep in mind

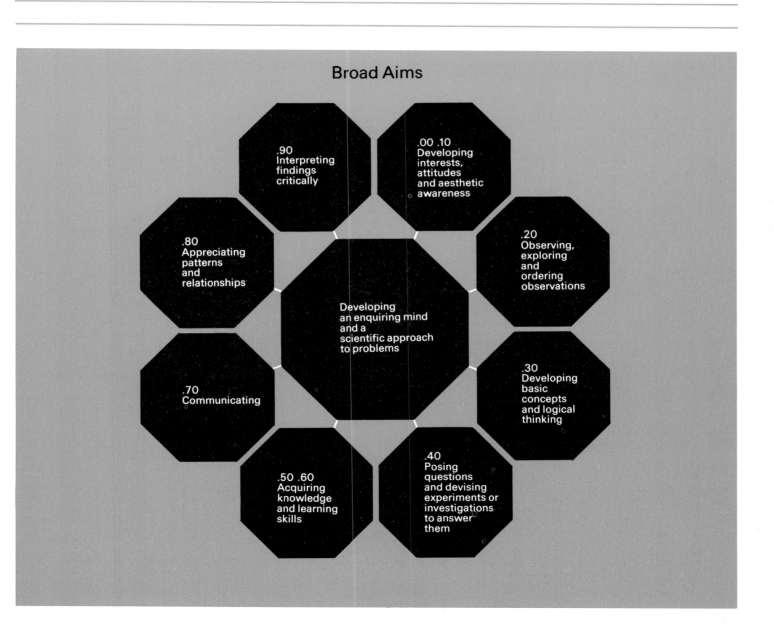

Broad Aims

.90 Interpreting findings critically

.00 .10 Developing interests, attitudes and aesthetic awareness

.80 Appreciating patterns and relationships

.20 Observing, exploring and ordering observations

Developing an enquiring mind and a scientific approach to problems

.70 Communicating

.30 Developing basic concepts and logical thinking

.50 .60 Acquiring knowledge and learning skills

.40 Posing questions and devising experiments or investigations to answer them

What we mean by Stage 1, Stage 2 and Stage 3

Attitudes, interests and aesthetic awareness

.00/.10

Stage 1
Transition from intuition to concrete operations. Infants generally.

The characteristics of thought among infant children differ in important respects from those of children over the age of about seven years. Infant thought has been described as 'intuitive' by Piaget; it is closely associated with physical action and is dominated by immediate observation. Generally, the infant is not able to think about or imagine the consequences of an action unless he has actually carried it out, nor is he yet likely to draw logical conclusions from his experiences. At this early stage the objectives are those concerned with active exploration of the immediate environment and the development of ability to discuss and communicate effectively: they relate to the kind of activities that are appropriate to these very young children, and which form an introduction to ways of exploring and of ordering observations.

1.01 Willingness to ask questions
1.02 Willingness to handle both living and non-living material.
1.03 Sensitivity to the need for giving proper care to living things.
1.04 Enjoyment in using all the senses for exploring and discriminating.
1.05 Willingness to collect material for observation or investigation.

Concrete operations. Early stage.

In this Stage, children are developing the ability to manipulate things mentally. At first this ability is limited to objects and materials that can be manipulated concretely, and even then only in a restricted way. The objectives here are concerned with developing these mental operations through exploration of concrete objects and materials—that is to say, objects and materials which, as physical things, have meaning for the child. Since older children, and even adults prefer an introduction to new ideas and problems through concrete example and physical exploration, these objectives are suitable for all children, whatever their age, who are being introduced to certain science activities for the first time.

1.06 Desire to find out things for oneself.
1.07 Willing participation in group work.
1.08 Willing compliance with safety regulations in handling tools and equipment.
1.09 Appreciation of the need to learn the meaning of new words and to use them correctly.

Stage 2
Concrete operations. Later stage.

In this Stage, a continuation of what Piaget calls the stage of concrete operations, the mental manipulations are becoming more varied and powerful. The developing ability to handle variables—for example, in dealing with multiple classification—means that problems can be solved in more ordered and quantitative ways than was previously possible. The objectives begin to be more specific to the exploration of the scientific aspects of the environment rather than to general experience, as previously. These objectives are developments of those of Stage 1 and depend on them for a foundation. They are those thought of as being appropriate for all children who have progressed from Stage 1 and not merely for nine- to eleven-year-olds.

2.01 Willingness to co-operate with others in science activities.
2.02 Willingness to observe objectively.
2.03 Appreciation of the reasons for safety regulations.
2.04 Enjoyment in examining ambiguity in the use of words.
2.05 Interest in choosing suitable means of expressing results and observations.
2.06 Willingness to assume responsibility for the proper care of living things.
2.07 Willingness to examine critically the results of their own and others' work.
2.08 Preference for putting ideas to test before accepting or rejecting them.
2.09 Appreciation that approximate methods of comparison may be more appropriate than careful measurements.

Stage 3
Transition to stage of abstract thinking.

This is the Stage in which, for some children, the ability to think about abstractions is developing. When this development is complete their thought is capable of dealing with the possible and hypothetical, and is not tied to the concrete and to the here and now. It may take place between eleven and thirteen for some able children, for some children it may happen later, and for others it may never occur. The objectives of this stage are ones which involve development of ability to use hypothetical reasoning and to separate and combine variables in a systematic way. They are appropriate to those who have achieved most of the Stage 2 objectives and who now show signs of ability to manipulate mentally ideas and propositions.

3.01 Acceptance of responsibility for their own and others' safety in experiments.
3.02 Preference for using words correctly.
3.03 Commitment to the idea of physical cause and effect.
3.04 Recognition of the need to standardise measurements.
3.05 Willingness to examine evidence critically.
3.06 Willingness to consider beforehand the usefulness of the results from a possible experiment.
3.07 Preference for choosing the most appropriate means of expressing results or observations.
3.08 Recognition of the need to acquire new skills.
3.09 Willingness to consider the role of science in everyday life.

Attitudes, interests and aesthetic awareness

.00/.10

Observing, exploring and ordering observations
.20

1.21 Appreciation of the variety of living things and materials in the environment.
1.22 Awareness of changes which take place as time passes.
1.23 Recognition of common shapes—square, circle, triangle.
1.24 Recognition of regularity in patterns.
1.25 Ability to group things consistently according to chosen or given criteria.

1.11 Awareness that there are various ways of testing out ideas and making observations.
1.12 Interest in comparing and classifying living or non-living things.
1.13 Enjoyment in comparing measurements with estimates.
1.14 Awareness that there are various ways of expressing results and observations.
1.15 Willingness to wait and to keep records in order to observe change in things.
1.16 Enjoyment in exploring the variety of living things in the environment.
1.17 Interest in discussing and comparing the aesthetic qualities of materials.

1.26 Awareness of the structure and form of living things.
1.27 Awareness of change of living things and non-living materials.
1.28 Recognition of the action of force
1.29 Ability to group living and non-living things by observable attributes.
1.29a Ability to distinguish regularity in events and motion.

2.11 Enjoyment in developing methods for solving problems or testing ideas.
2.12 Appreciation of the part that aesthetic qualities of materials play in determining their use.
2.13 Interest in the way discoveries were made in the past.

2.21 Awareness of internal structure in living and non-living things.
2.22 Ability to construct and use keys for identification.
2.23 Recognition of similar and congruent shapes.
2.24 Awareness of symmetry in shapes and structures.
2.25 Ability to classify living things and non-living materials in different ways.
2.26 Ability to visualise objects from different angles and the shape of cross-sections.

3.11 Appreciation of the main principles in the care of living things.
3.12 Willingness to extend methods used in science activities to other fields of experience.

3.21 Appreciation that classification criteria are arbitrary.
3.22 Ability to distinguish observations which are relevant to the solution of a problem from those which are not.
3.23 Ability to estimate the order of magnitude of physical quantities.

	Developing basic concepts and logical thinking .30	**Posing questions and devising experiments or investigations to answer them** .40
Stage 1 Transition from intuition to concrete operations. Infants generally.	1.31 Awareness of the meaning of words which describe various types of quantity. 1.32 Appreciation that things which are different may have features in common.	1.41 Ability to find answers to simple problems by investigation. 1.42 Ability to make comparisons in terms of one property or variable.
Concrete operations. Early stage.	1.33 Ability to predict the effect of certain changes through observation of similar changes. 1.34 Formation of the notions of the horizontal and the vertical. 1.35 Development of concepts of conservation of length and substance. 1.36 Awareness of the meaning of speed and of its relation to distance covered.	1.43 Appreciation of the need for measurement. 1.44 Awareness that more than one variable may be involved in a particular change.
Stage 2 Concrete operations. Later stage.	2.31 Appreciation of measurement as division into regular parts and repeated comparison with a unit. 2.32 Appreciation that comparisons can be made indirectly by use of an intermediary. 2.33 Development of concepts of conservation of weight, area and volume. 2.34 Appreciation of weight as a downward force. 2.35 Understanding of the speed, time, distance relation.	2.41 Ability to frame questions likely to be answered through investigations. 2.42 Ability to investigate variables and to discover effective ones. 2.43 Appreciation of the need to control variables and use controls in investigations. 2.44 Ability to choose and use either arbitrary or standard units of measurement as appropriate. 2.45 Ability to select a suitable degree of approximation and work to it. 2.46 Ability to use representational models for investigating problems or relationships.
Stage 3 Transition to stage of abstract thinking.	3.31 Familiarity with relationships involving velocity, distance, time, acceleration. 3.32 Ability to separate, exclude or combine variables in approaching problems. 3.33 Ability to formulate hypotheses not dependent upon direct observation. 3.34 Ability to extend reasoning beyond the actual to the possible. 3.35 Ability to distinguish a logically sound proof from others less sound.	3.41 Attempting to identify the essential steps in approaching a problem scientifically. 3.42 Ability to design experiments with effective controls for testing hypotheses. 3.43 Ability to visualise a hypothetical situation as a useful simplification of actual observations. 3.44 Ability to construct scale models for investigation and to appreciate implications of changing the scale.

1.51 Ability to discriminate between different materials.
1.52 Awareness of the characteristics of living things.
1.53 Awareness of properties which materials can have.
1.54 Ability to use displayed reference material for identifying living and non-living things.

1.55 Familiarity with sources of sound.
1.56 Awareness of sources of heat, light and electricity.
1.57 Knowledge that change can be produced in common substances.
1.58 Appreciation that ability to move or cause movement requires energy.
1.59 Knowledge of differences in properties between and within common groups of materials.

1.61 Appreciation of man's use of other living things and their products.
1.62 Awareness that man's way of life has changed through the ages.
1.63 Skill in manipulating tools and materials.
1.64 Development of techniques for handling living things correctly.
1.65 Ability to use books for supplementing ideas or information.

2.51 Knowledge of conditions which promote changes in living things and non-living materials.
2.52 Familiarity with a wide range of forces and of ways in which they can be changed.
2.53 Knowledge of sources and simple properties of common forms of energy.
2.54 Knowledge of the origins of common materials.
2.55 Awareness of some discoveries and inventions by famous scientists.
2.56 Knowledge of ways to investigate and measure properties of living things and non-living materials.
2.57 Awareness of changes in the design of measuring instruments and tools during man's history.
2.58 Skill in devising and constructing simple apparatus.
2.59 Ability to select relevant information from books or other reference material.

3.51 Knowledge that chemical change results from interaction.
3.52 Knowledge that energy can be stored and converted in various ways.
3.53 Awareness of the universal nature of gravity.
3.54 Knowledge of the main constituents and variations in the composition of soil and of the earth.
3.55 Knowledge that properties of matter can be explained by reference to its particulate nature.
3.56 Knowledge of certain properties of heat, light, sound, electrical, mechanical and chemical energy.
3.57 Knowledge of a wide range of living organisms.
3.58 Development of the concept of an internal environment.
3.59 Knowledge of the nature and variations in basic life processes.

3.61 Appreciation of levels of organisation in living things.
3.62 Appreciation of the significance of the work and ideas of some famous scientists.
3.63 Ability to apply relevant knowledge without help of contextual cues.
3.64 Ability to use scientific equipment and instruments for extending the range of human senses.

Communicating	Appreciating patterns and relationships
.70	.80

Stage 1
Transition from intuition to concrete operations. Infants generally.

1.71 Ability to use new words appropriately.
1.72 Ability to record events in their sequences.
1.73 Ability to discuss and record impressions of living and non-living things in the environment.
1.74 Ability to use representational symbols for recording information on charts or block graphs.

1.81 Awareness of cause-effect relationships.

Concrete operations. Early stage.

1.75 Ability to tabulate information and use tables.
1.76 Familiarity with names of living things and non-living materials.
1.77 Ability to record impressions by making models, painting or drawing.

1.82 Development of a concept of environment.
1.83 Formation of a broad idea of variation in living things.
1.84 Awareness of seasonal changes in living things.
1.85 Awareness of differences in physical conditions between different parts of the Earth.

Stage 2
Concrete operations. Later stage.

2.71 Ability to use non-representational symbols in plans, charts, etc.
2.72 Ability to interpret observations in terms of trends and rates of change.
2.73 Ability to use histograms and other simple graphical forms for communicating data.
2.74 Ability to construct models as a means of recording observations.

2.81 Awareness of sequences of change in natural phenomena.
2.82 Awareness of structure-function relationship in parts of living things.
2.83 Appreciation of interdependence among living things.
2.84 Awareness of the impact of man's activities on other living things.
2.85 Awareness of the changes in the physical environment brought about by man's activity.
2.86 Appreciation of the relationships of parts and wholes.

Stage 3
Transition to stage of abstract thinking.

3.71 Ability to select the graphical form most appropriate to the information being recorded.
3.72 Ability to use three-dimensional models or graphs for recording results.
3.73 Ability to deduce information from graphs: from gradient, area, intercept.
3.74 Ability to use analogies to explain scientific ideas and theories.

3.81 Recognition that the ratio of volume to surface area is significant.
3.82 Appreciation of the scale of the universe.
3.83 Understanding of the nature and significance of changes in living and non-living things.
3.84 Recognition that energy has many forms and is conserved when it is changed from one form to another.
3.85 Recognition of man's impact on living things— conservation, change, control.
3.86 Appreciation of the social implications of man's changing use of materials, historical and contemporary.
3.87 Appreciation of the social implications of research in science.
3.88 Appreciation of the role of science in the changing pattern of provision for human needs.

0

91 Awareness that the apparent size, shape and relationships
of things depend on the position of the observer.

- -

.92 Appreciation that properties of materials influence their
use.

2.91 Appreciation of adaptation to environment.
2.92 Appreciation of how the form and structure of materials
relate to their function and properties.
2.93 Awareness that many factors need to be considered when
choosing a material for a particular use.
2.94 Recognition of the role of chance in making measurements
and experiments.

These Stages we have chosen conform
to modern ideas about children's learning.
They conveniently describe for us the
mental development of children between the
ages of five and thirteen years, but it must
be remembered that ALTHOUGH
CHILDREN GO THROUGH THESE STAGES
IN THE SAME ORDER THEY DO NOT
GO THROUGH THEM AT THE SAME
RATES.
SOME children achieve the later Stages at an
early age.
SOME loiter in the early Stages for quite a time.
SOME never have the mental ability to
develop to the later Stages.
ALL appear to be ragged in their movement
from one Stage to another.
Our Stages, then, are not tied to
chronological age, so in any one class of
children there will be, almost certainly, some
children at differing Stages of mental
development.

3.91 Ability to draw from observations conclusions that are
unbiased by preconception.
3.92 Willingness to accept factual evidence despite preceptual
contradictions.
3.93 Awareness that the degree of accuracy of measurements
has to be taken into account when results are interpreted.
3.94 Awareness that unstated assumptions can affect
conclusions drawn from argument or experimental results.
3.95 Appreciation of the need to integrate findings into a
simplifying generalisation.
3.96 Willingness to check that conclusions are consistent with
further evidence.

97

Index

Illustration acknowledgements:

The publishers gratefully acknowledge the help given by the
following in supplying photographs on the pages indicated:

Ardea Photographs, 77
British Concrete Corporation, 49
British Ropes Limited, 47
British Steel Corporation, 18
Canadian High Commissioner, 16
Cambridge City Libraries, 39
Cheshire Education Committee, 22
CIBA (A.R.L.) Limited, 65
The Gas Council, 55
The Institute of Geological Sciences, 81
International Paper Company, New York, 14
Kinnear Moodie & Company Limited, 8
Natural History Photographic Agency, 79, 80, 84
Robin Laurence, 3
Southwest Picture Agency, 15, 68
The Swiss National Tourist Office, 24
United States Information Service, 2
Line drawings by The Garden Studio: Corinne Clark

Cover design by Peter Gauld